LEARN TO
Knit Lace

Buttercup Baby Set, page 58

www.companyscoming.com
visit our ✦ website

Rosebuds Throw, page 86

Learn to Knit Lace

Copyright © Company's Coming Publishing Limited

First Printing April 2012

Library and Archives Canada Cataloguing in Publication
Learn to knit lace.
(Workshop series)
Includes index.
ISBN 978-1-897477-76-2
1. Knitted lace. 2. Lace and lace making. 3. Knitting.
I. Title: Knit lace. II. Series: Workshop series (Edmonton, Alta.)
TT805.K54L43 2012   746.2'26   C2011-906146-5

Published by
Company's Coming Publishing Limited
2311-96 Street
Edmonton, Alberta, Canada T6N 1G3
Tel: 780-450-6223 Fax: 780-450-1857
www.companyscoming.com

Company's Coming is a registered trademark owned by Company's Coming Publishing Limited

Printed in China

The Company's Coming Story

Jean Paré grew up with an understanding that family, friends and home cooking are the key ingredients for a good life. A mother of four, Jean worked as a professional caterer for 18 years, operating out of her home kitchen. During that time, she came to appreciate quick and easy recipes that call for everyday ingredients. In answer to mounting requests for her recipes, Company's Coming cookbooks were born, and Jean moved on to a new chapter in her career.

In the beginning, Jean worked from a spare bedroom in her home, located in the small prairie town of Vermilion, Alberta, Canada. The first Company's Coming cookbook, *150 Delicious Squares*, was an immediate bestseller. Today, with well over 150 titles in print, Company's Coming has earned the distinction of publishing Canada's most popular cookbooks. The company continues to gain new supporters by adhering to Jean's "Golden Rule of Cooking"—Never share a recipe you wouldn't use yourself. It's an approach that has worked—millions of times over!

Company's Coming cookbooks are distributed throughout Canada, the United States, Australia and other international English-language markets. French and Spanish language editions have also been published. Sales to date have surpassed 30 million copies with no end in sight. Familiar and trusted in home kitchens around the world, Company's Coming cookbooks are highly regarded both as kitchen workbooks and as family heirlooms.

Company's Coming founder Jean Paré

Just as Company's Coming continues to promote the tradition of home cooking, the same is now true with crafting. Like good cooking, great craft results depend upon easy-to-follow instructions, readily available materials and enticing photographs of the finished products. Also like cooking, crafting is meant to be enjoyed in the home or cottage. Company's Coming Crafts, then, is a natural extension from the kitchen into the family room or den.

Because Company's Coming operates a test kitchen and not a craft shop, we've partnered with a major North American craft content publisher to assemble a variety of craft compilations exclusively for us. Our editors have been involved every step of the way. You can see the excellent results for yourself in the book you're holding.

Company's Coming Crafts are for everyone—whether you're a beginner or a seasoned pro. What better gift could you offer than something you've made yourself? In these hectic days, people still enjoy crafting parties; they bring family and friends together in the same way a good meal does. Company's Coming is proud to support crafters with this new creative book series.

We hope you enjoy these easy-to-follow, informative and colourful books, and that they inspire your creativity. So, don't delay—get crafty!

TABLE OF CONTENTS

First Steps

Begin your lace knitting adventure with these easy projects for you or your home.

Cables & Lace Dishcloth, 30

Suri Lace Scarf, 34

Simple Lace Top, 51

Catching On

Now it is time to try adding shape to your lace knitting with a simple cowl or sweater.

Easy Lace Cowl, 46

TABLE OF CONTENTS

Gaining Confidence

This chapter is full of accessories for you—a shawl or bag, and accents for your home as well.

Branching Out

Now it is time to move on to sweaters and baby layettes!

Lacy Leaves Tunic, 94

Lace Shopping Bag, 81

Springtime Beret, 67

Ziggy's Ensemble, 104

Make it yourself!

COLLECT THEM ALL!

Kids Learn To Knit, Quilt And Crochet
Learn To Bead Earrings
Learn To Bead Jewellery
Learn To Craft With Paper
Learn To Crochet For Baby
Learn To Crochet In A Day
Learn To Knit For Baby
Learn To Knit In The Round
Learn To Knit Socks
Learn To Make Cards With Folds
Learn To Make Cards With Photos
Learn To Quilt Fat Quarters
Learn To Quilt With Panels
Learn To Sew For The Table

CRAFT WORKSHOP SERIES

Get a craft class in a book! General instructions
teach basic skills or how to apply them in a new
way. Easy-to-follow steps, diagrams and photos
make projects simple.

Whether paper crafting, knitting, crocheting,
beading, sewing or quilting—find beautiful, fun
designs you can make yourself.

Look for Company's Coming cookbooks and craft books in stores or order them on-line at
www.companyscoming.com

FOREWORD

As you move through the chapters of *Learn to Knit Lace*— First Steps, Catching On, Gaining Confidence and Branching Out—you will quickly and easily advance your knitting skills.

The Knitting Basics introduction ends with some basic instructions on how to read a chart, the "First Steps" to knitting lace. Create simple yet beautiful accents to any outfit from casual to formal. These first steps offer lace accents for you and your home, from wraps to afghans. Add lacy to everything you touch.

Now that you are "Catching On" to lace knitting, you can add some shaping skills. You will be surprised at how easy it is to move from the simplicity of a scarf to the details of a sweater. In this chapter you will see that you have the skills to knit for family members of any age. Natural Beauty for Baby and Easy Lace Cowl will impress not just yourself but also the grateful recipients of these simple, beautiful pieces.

Now that you are "Gaining Confidence," it is time to expand your knitting skills. Try a double yarn over with the Garter Diamonds Shawl. Broaden your horizons with the repeating patterns of the Japanese Lace Vest. The next time you take a meal to a friend in need, top it with the lasting gift of a Bread-Basket Lace Cover or Lace Star Candle Mat and turn a quick gift into a family heirloom. If a small, quick gift isn't enough for a housewarming, our Rosebuds Throw is the perfect accent to any home.

It is time for "Branching Out." How do you tell that special friend or family member just how much she means to you? Ziggy's Ensemble or Diagonal Eyelets Baby Set will reflect those untold sentiments. And what says "I Love You" like hand-knit socks? But remember to take time to pamper yourself with a lacy tunic or cardigan.

Pick up some knitting needles and yarn and learn to knit lace!

Make Mine Colourful Throw, page 44

KNITTING BASICS

Getting Started

Supplies Needed for Practice Lessons

3½ oz skein of worsted weight yarn in a light colour

Size 8 (5mm) 10-inch-long straight knitting needles

Size H/8 (5mm) crochet hook (for repairs)

Scissors

Tape measure

Size 16 tapestry needle or plastic yarn needle

Later on, for some of the projects in this book, you can add all kinds of accessories such as stitch markers, stitch holders and needle point protectors. But for now, you only need the items listed above.

Yarn

Yarn comes in a wonderful selection of fibres, ranging from wool to metallic, textures from lumpy to smooth, colours from the palest pastels to vibrant neon shades and weights from gossamer fine to chunky.

The most commonly used yarn, and the one you'll need for the lessons in this book, is worsted weight (sometimes called medium weight or 4-ply). It is readily available in a wide variety of beautiful colours. Choose a light colour for practice—it will be much easier to see the individual stitches.

Always read yarn labels carefully for information including the following: how much yarn is in the skein, hank or ball, in ounces or grams and in yards or metres; the type of yarn; how to care for it; and sometimes how to pull the yarn from the skein (and yes, there is a trick to this!). The label usually bears a dye-lot number, which assures you that the colour of each skein with this same number is identical. The same colour name may vary from dye lot to dye lot, creating unsightly variations in colour when a project is finished—so when purchasing yarn for a project, be sure to match the dye-lot number on the skeins and purchase enough to complete the project.

You'll need a blunt-point tapestry or yarn needle with an eye big enough to carry the yarn for weaving in ends and joining pieces. You can use a size 16 steel tapestry needle or purchase a large plastic sewing needle called a yarn needle.

Crochet Hooks

Even though you're knitting, not crocheting, you'll need to have a crochet hook handy for correcting mistakes, retrieving dropped stitches and for some finishing techniques. (You don't need previous experience with crochet—only the simplest crochet stitch is normally used when finishing edges!)

The hook size you need depends on the thickness of the yarn you are using for your project, and on the size of the knitting needles.

Here's a handy chart to show you what size hook to use:

Knitting Needle Size	Crochet Hook Size
5, 6	F
7, 8, 9	G
10 and 10½	H
11 and 13	I
15 and 17	J

Knitting Needles

Most knitting needles come in pairs of straight needles, each with a shaped point at one end and a knob at the other end so that the stitches won't slide off. Needles also come in sets of four double-point needles used for making small seamless projects, and in circular form with a point at each end.

You will most often use straight needles, which are readily available in many materials including aluminum, bamboo and plastic. Straight needles come in a variety of lengths, the most common being 10 inches and 14 inches. For our lessons, we will use the 10-inch length.

Needles also come in a variety of sizes, which refer to the diameter and thus the size of the stitch you can make with them. These are numbered from 0 (the smallest usually available) to 17 (the largest usually available). There are larger needles, but they are not used as often. For our lessons, we use a size 8 needle, an average size for use with worsted weight yarn.

Let's look at a knitting needle:

point   shaft

Now, with your yarn and needles ready, let's get started.

Lesson 1

Casting On

Knitting always starts with a row of foundation stitches worked onto one needle. Making a foundation row is called casting on. Although there are several ways of casting on, the following way is the easiest for beginners:

1. Make a slip knot on one needle as follows: Make a yarn loop, leaving about 4-inch length of yarn at free end.

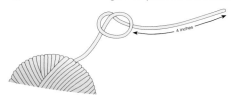

Insert knitting needle into loop and draw up yarn from free end to make a loop on needle.

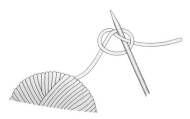

Pull yarn firmly, but not tightly, to form a slip knot on the shaft, not the point, of the needle. Pull yarn end to tighten the loop. This slip knot counts as your first stitch.

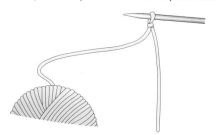

2. Place the needle with the knot in your left hand, placing the thumb and index finger close to the point of the needle, which helps you control it.

3. Hold the other needle with your right hand, again with your fingers close to the point. Grasp the needle firmly, but not tightly.

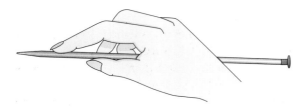

4. Your right hand controls the yarn coming from the ball. To help keep your tension even, hold the yarn loosely against the palm of your hand with three fingers, then up and over your index finger. These diagrams show how this looks from above the hand and beneath the hand.

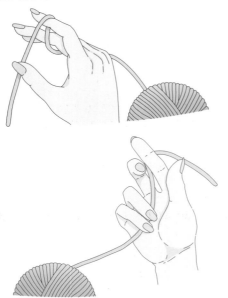

5. Insert the point of the right needle—from front to back—into the slip knot and under the left needle.

6. Continuing to hold the left needle in your left hand, move your left fingers over to brace the right needle.

With your right index finger, pick up the yarn from the ball,

and releasing your right hand's grip on the right needle, bring yarn under and over the point of the right needle.

7. Returning your right fingers to the right needle, draw the yarn through the stitch with the right needle.

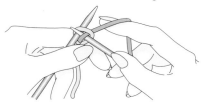

8. Slide the left needle point into the new stitch, and then remove right needle.

9. Pull the ball of yarn gently, but not tightly, to make the stitch snug on the needle; you should be able to slip the stitch back and forth on the shaft of the needle easily.

You have now made one stitch, and there are two stitches on the left needle (remember the slip knot counts as a stitch).

10. Insert the point of the right needle—from front to back—into the stitch you've just made and under the left needle.

Repeat steps 6 through 10 for the next stitch.

Continue repeating steps 6 through 10 until you have 24 stitches on the left needle. Be sure to pull each stitch up, off the point and onto the shaft of the left needle.

Lesson 2

The Knit Stitch

All knitting is made up of only two basic stitches, the knit stitch and the purl stitch. These are combined in many ways to create different effects and textures. That means you're halfway to being a knitter, since you already learned the knit stitch as you practiced casting on! The first three steps of the knit stitch are exactly like casting on.

1. Hold the needle with the 24 cast-on stitches from Lesson 1 in your left hand. Insert the point of the right needle in the first stitch, from front to back, just as in casting on.

2. With your right index finger, bring yarn from the skein under and over the point of the right needle.

3. Draw yarn through the stitch with the right needle point.

4. The next step now differs from casting on. Slip the loop on the left needle off, so the new stitch is entirely on the right needle.

Now you've completed your first knit stitch! Repeat these four steps in each stitch remaining on the left needle. When all stitches are on the right needle and the left needle is free, another row has been completed. Turn the right needle and place it in your left hand. Hold the free needle in your right hand. Work another row of stitches in same manner as last row, taking care not to work too tightly. Work 10 more rows of knit stitches.

The pattern formed by knitting every row is called garter stitch and looks the same on both sides. When counting rows in garter stitch, each raised ridge indicates you have knitted two rows.

Tip: When working on a garter stitch project it is helpful to place a small safety pin on the right side of the piece, because after a few rows both sides look the same.

Lesson 3

The Purl Stitch

The reverse of the knit stitch is called the purl stitch. Instead of inserting the right needle point from front to back under the left needle (as you did for the knit stitch), you will now insert it from back to front, in front of the left needle. Work as follows on the 24 stitches already on your needle.

1. Insert the right needle, from right to left, into the first stitch and in front of the left needle.

2. Holding the yarn in front of the work (side toward you), bring it around the right needle counterclockwise.

3. With the right needle, pull the yarn back through the stitch.

4. Slide the stitch off the left needle, leaving the new stitch on the right needle.

Your first purl stitch is now completed. Continue to repeat these four steps in every stitch across the row. The row you have just purled will be considered the wrong side of your work for the moment.

Now transfer the needle with the stitches from your right to left hand; the side of the work now facing you is called the right side of your work. Knit every stitch in the row; at end of row, transfer the needle with the stitches to your left hand, then purl every stitch in the row. Knit across another row, then purl across another row.

Now stop and look at your work; by alternating knit and purl rows, you are creating one of the most frequently used stitch patterns in knitting, stockinette stitch.

Turn the work over to the right side; it should look like stitches in Photo A. The wrong side of the work should look like stitches in Photo B.

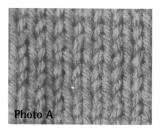
Photo A

Photo B

Continue with your practice piece, alternately knitting and purling rows, until you feel comfortable with the needles and yarn. As you work you'll see that your piece will begin to look more even.

Tip: Hold your work and hands in a comfortable relaxed position. The more comfortable and relaxed you are, the more even your work will be.

Lesson 4

Correcting Mistakes

Dropped Stitches
Each time you knit or purl a stitch, take care to pull the stitch off the left needle after completing the new stitch. Otherwise, you will be adding stitches when you don't

want to. If you let a stitch slip off the needle before you've knitted or purled it, it's called a dropped stitch. Even expert knitters drop a stitch now and then, but an unintentionally dropped stitch must be picked up and put back on the needle. If not, the stitch will "run" down the length of the piece, just like a run in a stocking!

If you notice the dropped stitch right away, and it has not run down more than one row, you can usually place it back on the needle easily.

But if it has dropped several rows, you'll find it easier to use a crochet hook to work the stitch back up to the needle.

On the knit side (right side of work) of the stockinette stitch, insert the crochet hook into the dropped stitch from front to back, under the horizontal strand in the row above.

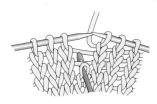

Hook the horizontal strand above and pull through the loop on the crochet hook. Continue in this manner until you reach the last row worked, and then transfer the loop from the crochet hook to the left needle, being careful not to twist it.

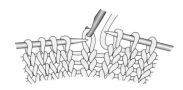

Unravelling Stitches

Sometimes it is necessary to unravel a large number of stitches, even down several rows, to correct a mistake. Whenever possible, carefully unravel the stitches one by one by putting the needle into the row below and undoing the stitch above, until the mistake is reached.

If several rows need to be unravelled, carefully slide all stitches off the needle and unravel each row down to the row in which the error occurred. Then unravel this row, stitch by stitch, placing each stitch, without twisting it, back on the needle in the correct position.

Lesson 5

Binding Off

Now you've learned how to cast on, knit and purl the stitches; next, you need to know how to take the stitches off the needle once you've finished a piece.

The process used to secure the stitches is called binding off. Let's bind off your practice piece; be careful to work loosely for this procedure and begin with the right side (the knit side) of your work facing you.

Knit Bind-Off

1. Knit the first two stitches. Now insert the left needle into the first of the two stitches, the one you knitted first,

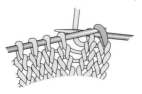

and pull it over the second stitch and completely off the needle. You have now bound off one stitch.

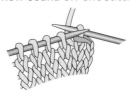

2. Knit one more stitch; insert the left needle into the first stitch on the right needle and pull the first stitch over the new stitch and completely off the needle. Another stitch is now bound off.

Repeat step 2 four times more; now knit each of the remaining stitches on the left needle. You should have 18 stitches on the right needle, and you have bound off six stitches on the knit side of your work. *Note: The first of the 18 stitches was worked while binding off the last stitch at the beginning of the row.*

To bind off on the purl side, turn your practice piece so the wrong side of your work is facing you.

Purl Bind-Off

1. Purl the first two stitches. Now insert the left needle into the first stitch on the right needle,

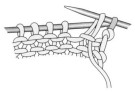

and pull it over the 2nd stitch and completely off the needle. You have now bound off one stitch.

2. Purl one more stitch; insert the left needle into the first stitch on the right needle and pull the first stitch over the new stitch and completely off the needle. Another stitch is bound off.

Repeat step 2 four times more; now purl each of the 11 stitches remaining on the left needle for a total of 12 stitches on the right needle.

Turn your work so that the right side is facing you; bind off six stitches in the same manner that you bound off the first six stitches on this side, and then knit remaining stitches.

Turn your work and bind off the remaining stitches on the wrong side; there will be one stitch left on the needle, and you are ready to "finish off" or "end off" the yarn. To do this,

cut the yarn leaving about a 6-inch end. With the needle, draw this end up through the final stitch to secure it.

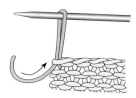

You have just learned to bind off knit stitches on the right side of your work and purl stitches on the wrong side of your work. When you wish to bind off in a pattern stitch, where some stitches in a row have been knitted and others purled, knit the knit stitches and purl the purl stitches as you work across the row.

Always bind off loosely to maintain the same amount of stretch or "give" at the edge as in the rest of your work. If the bind off is too tight at the neckband ribbing of a pullover sweater, for example, the sweater will not fit over your head!

Tip: You can ensure the binding off being loose enough if you replace the needle in your right hand with a needle one size larger.

Lesson 6

Increasing

To shape knitted pieces, you will make them wider or narrower by increasing or decreasing a certain number of stitches from time to time.

Begin a new practice piece by casting on 12 stitches. Work four rows of garter stitch (remember this means you will knit every row); then on the next row, purl across (this purl side now becomes the wrong side of the work, since you will now begin working in stockinette stitch). Knit one more row, then purl one more row. You are now ready to practice increasing.

Although there are many ways to increase, this method is used most often.

Knit (or Purl) Two Stitches in One

1. On your practice piece (with the right side facing you), work as follows in the first stitch:

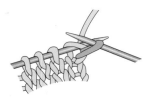

2. Insert the tip of the right needle from front to back into the stitch, and knit it in the usual manner, but don't remove the stitch from the left needle.

Insert the needle, from front to back, into the back loop of the same stitch, and knit it again, this time slipping the stitch off the left needle. You have now increased one stitch.

Knit across the row until one stitch remains, and then increase again by repeating steps 1 and 2. You should now have 14 stitches.

Purl one row and then knit one row, without increasing.

On your next row, the purl side, again increase in the first stitch. To increase on the purl side, insert the needle, from back to front, into the stitch; purl the stitch in the usual manner but don't remove it from the left needle. Then insert the needle, from back to front, into the back loop of the same stitch;

purl it again, this time slipping the stitch off. Then purl across to the last stitch; increase again. You should now have 16 stitches.

Now knit one row and purl one row without increasing.

Lesson 7

Decreasing

Method 1: Right Slanting Decrease

Knit (or Purl) Two Stitches Together (k2tog/p2tog)
In this method, you simply knit two stitches as one. Knit the first stitch on your practice piece, and then decrease as follows:

1. Insert the needle in the usual manner but through the fronts of the next two stitches on the left needle.

2. Bring yarn under and over the point of the needle and draw the yarn through both stitches.

Slip the stitches off the left needle. One new stitch will be on the right needle.

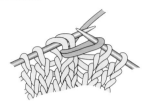

You have decreased one stitch. Knit across to the last three stitches; repeat steps 1 and 2 again to decrease another stitch, and then knit the last stitch. You should now have 14 stitches.

This decrease can also be worked on the purl side. On the next row of your practice piece, purl one stitch, and then insert the needle in the fronts of the next two stitches and purl them as if they were one stitch. Purl to the last three stitches, decrease again; purl the remaining stitch.

Method 2: Left Slanting Decrease

Pass Slipped Stitch Over (psso)

This method is often used in the shaping of raglans or other pieces where a definite decrease line is desired. In the following samples the decrease is worked one stitch in from the edge. By working in one stitch from the edge, the decrease does not become a part of the seam.

To use this method you must first know how to "slip" a stitch. When instructions say to slip a stitch, this means you will slip it from the left needle to the right, without working it. Usually when you slip a stitch, you will slip it as if to purl. However, when decreasing, you will always slip stitches as if to knit. Insert the right needle into the next stitch as if you were going to knit it, but don't work the stitch; just slip it from the left needle to the right needle.

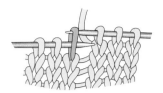

Now that you know how to slip a stitch, you can practice the second method of decreasing. On your practice piece, knit the first stitch. Instructions to decrease may read: "Slip 1, knit 1, pass slipped stitch over." (Sl 1, k1, psso.) To do this, work as follows:

1. Slip the next stitch, as if to knit.

2. Knit the next stitch.

3. Pass the slipped stitch over the knitted stitch by using the point of the left needle to lift the slipped stitch over the next stitch and completely off the needle.

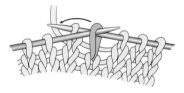

Knit to the last three stitches. Repeat steps 1 through 3. Then knit the last stitch.

This decrease can also be worked on the purl side. Purl two stitches, slip one stitch knitwise, pass the last 2 stitches back to the left-hand needle, then lift the slipped stitch over the purled stitch and off the needle.

Decreasing, Alternate Method 2: Left Slanting Decrease

Slip, Slip, Knit (ssk)

This decrease is similar in appearance to the previous method but has a smoother look since the stitch is not lifted or pulled up causing a slightly larger loop.

When this decrease is used, the stitches are slipped as if to **knit**.

1. To practice this method, knit the first stitch, slip the next two stitches one at a time from the left to the right needle as if to knit.

2. Insert the left needle into the back of both stitches, bring the yarn around the needle as if knitting and lift the two stitches over and off the left needle at the same time.

Knit to the last three stitches, repeat the slip, slip, knit the two slipped stitches together, and then knit the last stitch. Purl one row.

Notice the two methods of decreasing. Method 1 causes the decreased stitch to slant from left to right, while in Method 2 the stitch slants from right to left. For a sweater, both methods are often used in the same row for a mirrored effect.

To practice this mirrored look, knit one stitch, decrease using either of the Method 2 decreases, knit to the last three stitches, knit two stitches together using Method 1 and knit the last stitch. Notice that both decreases slant towards the centre of your sample.

Lesson 8

Ribbing

Sometimes you want a piece of knitting to fit more closely—such as at the neck, wrists or bottom of a sweater. To do this, a combination of knit and purl stitches alternating in the same row, called ribbing, creates an elastic effect. To practice ribbing, start a new piece by casting on 24 stitches loosely. Always cast on loosely for ribbing to provide enough stretch in the first row.

Knit Two, Purl Two Ribbing

Pattern row: Knit two stitches, then bring yarn under the needle to the front of the work and purl two stitches; take the yarn under the needle to the back of the work and knit two stitches; yarn to front again, purl two stitches.

Note: You may tend to add stitches accidentally by forgetting to move the yarn to the front before purling, or to the back before knitting.

Remembering to move the yarn, repeat this knit two, purl two alternating pattern across the row.

Work this same Pattern row 11 more times or until you feel comfortable with it. Your work should look like this:

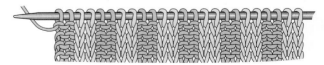

Tip: If you have trouble distinguishing a knit stitch from a purl stitch, remember that the smooth "V-shaped" stitches are knit stitches and the bumpy ones are purl stitches.

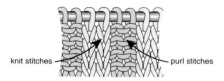

knit stitches — purl stitches

Bind off loosely, remembering to knit the knit (smooth) stitches and purl the purl (bumpy) stitches. Look at the work and see how the ribbing draws it in.

Knit One, Purl One Ribbing
This rib stitch pattern produces a finer ribbing and is often used on baby clothes or on garments knitted with light-weight yarns. Again cast on 24 stitches.

Pattern row: Knit the first stitch, yarn under needle to front, purl the next stitch; yarn under needle to back, knit next stitch; yarn to front, purl next stitch. Continue across row, alternating one knit stitch with one purl stitch.

Work this same Pattern row 11 more times or until you feel comfortable with this rib pattern. Your work should look like this:

Practice this ribbing for several more rows, then bind off in ribbing, knitting the knit (smooth) stitches and purling the purl (bumpy) stitches.

Lesson 9

Changing Yarn

Joining Yarn
New yarn should be added only at the beginning of a row, never in the middle of a row, unless this is required for a colour pattern change. To add yarn, tie the new strand around the old strand, making a knot at the edge of work, leaving at least a 4-inch end on both old and new strands. Then proceed to knit with the new yarn. The ends will be hidden later.

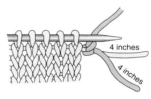

4 inches

4 inches

Carrying Yarn
When a yarn is repeated every several rows, it can be carried along the edge when not in use. At the beginning of the row, bring the carried colour under and over the colour just used and begin knitting (or purling).

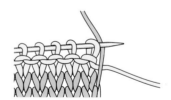

Lesson 10

Gauge & Measuring

This is the most important lesson of all, because if you don't work to gauge, your knitted garments will not fit as designed.

Gauge simply means the number of stitches per inch and the number of rows per inch that result from a specified yarn worked with needles in a specified size. This was the information used by the designer when creating the project.

But, since everyone knits differently—some loosely, some tightly, some in between—the measurements of individual work will vary greatly, even when the knitters use exactly the same pattern and exactly the same size yarn and needles.

That's why you need to knit a gauge swatch before you actually start working on a project.

Needle sizes given in instructions are merely guides and should never be used without making a 4-inch square sample swatch to check your gauge. *It is your responsibility to make sure you achieve the gauge specified in the pattern.* To achieve this gauge, you may need to use a different needle size—either larger or smaller—than that specified in the pattern. Always change to larger or smaller needles if necessary to achieve gauge.

Here's how to check your gauge. At the beginning of every knit pattern you'll find a gauge given, like this (note the use of abbreviations):

16 sts and 24 rows = 4 inches/10cm in St st, with size 8 needles.

This means that you will work your gauge swatch in stockinette stitch and will try to achieve a gauge of 16 stitches and 24 rows to 4 inches. You must make a gauge swatch at least 4 inches square to adequately test your work.

Starting with the recommended size 8 needle, cast on 16 stitches. Work in stockinette stitch for 24 rows. Loosely bind off all stitches.

Place the swatch on a flat surface and pin it out, being careful not to stretch it. Measure the outside edges; the swatch should be 4 inches square.

Now measure the centre 2 inches from side to side, and count the actual stitches. There should be eight stitches in the 2 inches.

8 stitches = 2 inches

Then measure the centre 2 inches from top to bottom and count the rows per inch. There should be 12 rows in the 2 inches.

If you have more stitches or rows per inch than specified, make another swatch with a size larger needles.

If you have fewer stitches or rows per inch than specified, make another swatch with a size smaller needles.

12 rows = 2 inches

Making gauge swatches before beginning a garment takes time and is a bother. But if you don't make the effort to do this important step, you'll never be able to create attractive, well-fitting garments.

Once you've begun a garment, it's a good idea to keep checking your gauge every few inches; if you become relaxed, you may find yourself knitting more loosely; if you tense up, your knitting may become tighter. To keep your gauge, it may be necessary to change needle sizes in the middle of a garment.

For a swatch in garter stitch, every two rows form a ridge which needs to be taken into consideration when counting rows.

2 rows

Lesson 11

Reading Patterns

Knitting patterns are written in a special language, full of abbreviations, asterisks, parentheses and other symbols and terms. These short forms are used so instructions will not take up too much space. They may seem confusing at first, but once understood, they are easy to follow.

Symbols

[ ] work instructions within brackets as many times as directed, such as [k2, p2] twice.

* repeat instructions following the * as directed; thus, "rep from * twice" means after working the instructions once, repeat the instructions following the asterisk twice more (three times in all).

( ) parentheses are used to list the garment sizes and to provide additional information to clarify instructions.

Work in established pattern is usually used when referring to a pattern stitch. The term means to continue following the pattern stitch as it is set up (established) on the needle. Work any subsequent increases or decreases in such a way that the established pattern remains the same (usually, working added stitches at the beginning or end of a row), outside the established pattern area.

Work even means to continue to work in the pattern as established, without working any increases or decreases.

Following Size in Patterns

The patterns for garments include a variety of sizes. Each pattern is written for the smallest size pattern with changes in the number of stitches (or inches) for other sizes in parentheses. For example, the pattern will tell you how many stitches to cast on as follows:

Cast on 20 (23, 24) stitches.

You would cast on 20 stitches for the smallest size, 23 stitches for the medium size and 24 stitches for the largest size. Depending on the pattern there may be more sizes or fewer sizes given. Check the measurements to determine the best size to make.

Before you begin knitting, it might be helpful to highlight or circle all the numbers for the size you are making throughout the pattern.

Lesson 12

Finishing

Many a well-knitted garment, worked exactly to gauge, ends up looking sloppy and amateurish simply because of bad finishing. Finishing a knitted garment requires no special skill, but it does require time, attention and knowledge of basic techniques.

Picking Up Stitches

You will often need to pick up a certain number of stitches along an edge, such as around a sweater neckline or armhole, so that ribbing or an edging can be worked. The pattern instructions will usually clearly state where and how many stitches to pick up. Although this is not difficult, it is often done incorrectly, and the results look messy. Many times a circular needle is used for picking up stitches.

For a neck edge, once the stitches are picked up, you begin knitting again in the first stitch and continue to work around the needle until the desired length is achieved.

To pick up a stitch, hold the knitting with the right side of the work facing you. Hold yarn from the skein behind the work, and hold a knitting needle in your right hand. Insert the point of the needle into the work from front to back, one stitch (at least two threads) from the edge; wrap the yarn around the needle as if knitting and draw the yarn through with the needle to the right side of the work making one stitch on the needle.

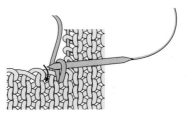

Pick up another stitch in the same manner, spacing stitches evenly along the edge.

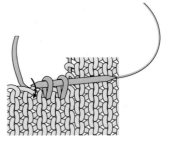

When picking up, pick up one stitch for each stitch when working across stitches in a horizontal row, and pick up about three stitches for every four rows when working along ends of rows. If a large number of stitches are to be picked up, it is best to mark off the edge into equal sections, and then pick up the same number of stitches in each section.

For stitches that have been bound off along a neck edge, pick up through both loops of each stitch.

Sometimes stitches are placed on a holder when working the front and back of a garment. When picking up these stitches they can either be knit directly from the holder or slipped to another needle and knit from it, depending on how they were originally slipped onto the holder.

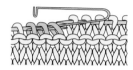

Blocking

Blocking simply means "setting" each piece into its final size and shape. (**Note:** *Be sure to check the yarn label before blocking, as some synthetic yarns and mohair yarns are ruined if they are blocked.*)

To block, moisten each piece first by dampening it with a light water spray. Then place each piece out on a padded flat surface (terry towelling provides adequate padding) right side up and away from direct sunlight. Referring to the small drawing or schematic in the pattern for the measurements for each piece, smooth out each piece to correct size and shape, using your fingers and the palms of your hands. Be sure to keep the stitches and rows in straight alignment. Use rustproof straight pins to hold the edges in place. Let pieces dry completely before removing.

If further blocking is required, use steam from a steam iron. Hold the iron close to the knitted piece and allow the steam to penetrate the fabric. Never rest the iron directly on the piece—knitting should never have a pressed flat look. Let dry completely before removing.

Important Note: *Never press ribbing, garter stitch, cables, or textured patterns such as those in Irish knits.*

Sewing Seams

Your pattern will usually tell you in what order to assemble the pieces. Use the same yarn as used in the garment to sew the seams, unless the yarn is too thick, in which case, use a thinner yarn in a matching colour.

Invisible Seam

This seam gives a smooth and neat appearance, as it weaves the edges together invisibly from the right side.

To join horizontal edges, such as shoulder seams, sew the edges together as shown below.

To join a front/back vertical edge to a horizontal sleeve edge, weave the edges together as shown below.

To join vertical edges, such as side seams or underarm sleeve seams, sew the edges together on the right side, pulling yarn gently until the edges meet as shown below.

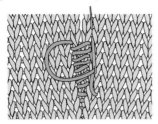

For pieces made using garter stitch, join vertical edges as shown below.

Tip: When seaming, do not draw the stitches too tight. The joining should have the same stretch or give as in the knitted garment.

Kitchener Stitch

This method of weaving with two needles is used for the toes of socks and flat seams. To weave the edges together and form an unbroken line of stockinette stitch, divide all stitches evenly onto two knitting needles—one behind the other. Thread yarn into tapestry needle. Hold needles with wrong sides of knit pieces together and work from right to left as follows:

1. Insert tapestry needle into first stitch on front needle as to purl. Draw yarn through stitch, leaving stitch on knitting needle.

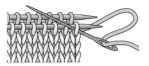

2. Insert tapestry needle into the first stitch on the back needle as to purl. Draw yarn through stitch and slip stitch off knitting needle.

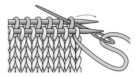

3. Insert tapestry needle into the next stitch on same (back) needle as to knit, leaving stitch on knitting needle.

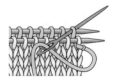

4. Insert tapestry needle into the first stitch on the front needle as to knit. Draw yarn through stitch and slip stitch off knitting needle.

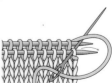

5. Insert tapestry needle into the next stitch on same (front) needle as to purl. Draw yarn through stitch, leaving stitch on knitting needle.

Repeat steps 2 through 5 until one stitch is left on each needle. Then repeat steps 2 and 4. Fasten off. Woven stitches should be the same size as adjacent knitted stitches.

Weaving in Ends
The final step is to weave in all the yarn ends securely. To do this, use a size 16 tapestry needle and weave the yarn ends through the backs of stitches.

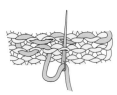

First weave the yarn about 2 inches in one direction and then 1 inch in the reverse direction. Cut off excess yarn.

If the ends are close to a seam, weave the yarn back and forth along the edge of the seam.

Lesson 13

Crochet Basics

Chain (ch)
Yo, pull through lp on hook.

Single Crochet (sc)
Insert the hook in the second chain through the centre of the V. Bring the yarn over the hook from back to front.

Draw the yarn through the chain stitch and onto the hook.

Again bring yarn over the hook from back to front and draw it through both loops on hook. For additional rows of single crochet, insert the hook under both loops of the previous stitch instead of through the centre of the V as when working into the chain stitch.

Reverse Single Crochet (reverse sc)
Chain 1 (a). Skip first stitch. Working from left to right, insert hook in next stitch from front to back (b), draw up loop on hook, yarn over, and draw through both loops on hook (c).

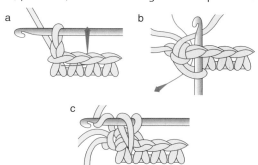

Lesson 14

Special Techniques

Here are some intermediate techniques for casting on and binding off. Try these once you are proficient in the basic techniques.

Long-Tail Cast-On

Begin with a length of yarn about three times the length of the finished cast-on edge. Make a slip knot, and place it on the needle. The yarn attached to the ball is the "working end," and the end created from the slip knot is the "long-tail end."

Hold the needle in one hand, and, with the other hand, create a "V" with your thumb and index finger. Hold the long-tail end in the crease of your thumb and the working yarn around your index finger.

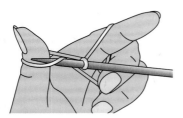

Swing the needle between the opening created under the thumb and the long-tail end, but do not release the yarn in the crease of your thumb.

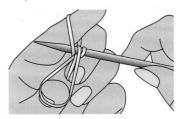

Wrap the working end around the needle, and use your thumb to pull the long-tail end up, over and off the needle as if to knit.

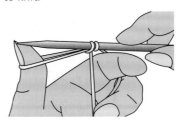

Remove your thumb, and tighten the long-tail end around the base of the stitch.

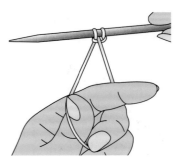

Repeat this process until you have the required number of stitches.

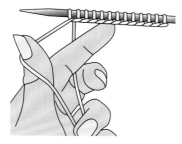

Cable Cast-On

Start with a slip knot placed on the left-hand needle, leaving a short tail. Pick up the right-hand needle, and knit one stitch.

Insert the right-hand needle between the two stitches, wrap the yarn over the needle and draw the yarn through the loop.

Place the new stitch onto the left-hand needle. Repeat this process until you have the required number of stitches.

3-Needle Bind-Off

Use this technique for seaming two edges together, such as when joining a shoulder seam. Hold the edge stitches on two separate needles with right sides together.

With a third needle, knit together a stitch from the front needle with one from the back.

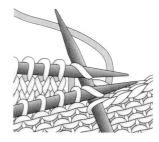

Repeat, knitting a stitch from the front needle with one from the back needle once more.

Slip the first stitch over the second.

Repeat, knitting a front and back pair of stitches together, and then bind one off.

Lesson 15

Reading Cable or Lace Symbols on a Chart

Charts are used to provide a visual image of the design, which is especially helpful when the row-by-row, written instructions would be very long and cumbersome to follow.

On a chart, each square represents a stitch. A stitch key is given to indicate what stitch the various symbols represent. For example, in the chart below, an empty square represents a stockinette stitch, so if you are working on the right side (RS), knit the stitch, and if you are working on the wrong side (WS), purl the stitch. A square with a dash represents a reverse stockinette stitch, so if you are working on the RS, purl the stitch, and if you are working on the WS, knit the stitch.

It is wise to check the stitch key and become familiar with the various symbols used on the chart before beginning the project.

The chart is read from bottom to top, and each row is numbered. For most charts, the right-side or odd-numbered rows are read across the chart from right to left; wrong-side or even-numbered rows are read from left to right. However, before beginning, check the placement of the row numbers on the chart.

Tips for Using Charts:

Enlarge a copy of the chart.

Use a magnetic board for the chart, moving a magnetic strip to mark your place but keeping the strip just above the row that you are about to work so that you can see how it coordinates with the previous rows. This will help you "read your knitting."

If the pattern is repeated only once, highlight the row once it is completed.

For a more complicated pattern, list the rows on a separate sheet of paper and check off rows as they are worked.

On that same sheet, make notes and keep track of the last row worked to avoid counting rows when you start your next knitting session.

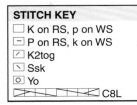

STITCH KEY
- ☐ K on RS, p on WS
- ⊟ P on RS, k on WS
- ☑ K2tog
- ◳ Ssk
- ⊙ Yo
- ▷▷◁◁ C8L

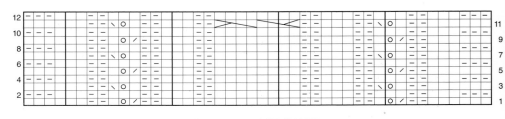

CABLES & LACE CHART

Standard Abbreviations

[ ] work instructions within brackets as many times as directed

( ) work instructions within parentheses in the place directed

** repeat instructions following the asterisks as directed

* repeat instructions following the single asterisk as directed

" inch(es)

approx approximately
beg begin/begins/beginning
CC contrasting colour
ch chain stitch
cm centimetre(s)

cn cable needle
dec decrease/decreases/ decreasing
dpn(s) double-point needle(s)
g gram(s)
inc increase/increases/increasing
k knit
k2tog knit 2 stitches together
kwise knitwise
LH left hand
m metre(s)
M1 make 1 stitch
MC main colour
mm millimetre(s)
oz ounce(s)
p purl

pat(s) pattern(s)
p2tog purl 2 stitches together
psso pass slipped stitch over
pwise purlwise
rem remain/remains/remaining
rep(s) repeat(s)
rev St st reverse stockinette stitch
RH right hand
rnd(s) rounds
RS right side
skp slip, knit, pass slipped stitch over—1 stitch decreased
sk2p slip 1, knit 2 together, pass slipped stitch over the knit 2 together—2 stitches decreased

sl slip
sl 1 kwise slip 1 knitwise
sl 1 pwise slip 1 purlwise
sl st slip stitch(es)
ssk slip, slip, knit these 2 stitches together—a decrease
st(s) stitch(es)
St st stockinette stitch
tbl through back loop(s)
tog together
WS wrong side
wyib with yarn in back
wyif with yarn in front
yd(s) yard(s)
yfwd yarn forward
yo (yo's) yarn over(s)

Standard Yarn Weight System

Categories of yarn, gauge ranges, and recommended needle sizes

Yarn Weight Symbol & Category Names	0 LACE	1 SUPER FINE	2 FINE	3 LIGHT	4 MEDIUM	5 BULKY	6 SUPER BULKY
Type of Yarns in Category	Fingering, 10-Count Crochet Thread	Sock, Fingering, Baby	Sport, Baby	DK, Light Worsted	Worsted, Afghan, Aran	Chunky, Craft, Rug	Bulky, Roving
Knit Gauge* Ranges in Stockinette Stitch to 4 inches	33–40 sts**	27–32 sts	23–26 sts	21–24 sts	16–20 sts	12–15 sts	6–11 sts
Recommended Needle in Metric Size Range	1.5–2.25mm	2.25–3.25mm	3.25–3.75mm	3.75–4.5mm	4.5–5.5mm	5.5–8mm	8mm
Recommended Needle U.S. Size Range	000 to 1	1 to 3	3 to 5	5 to 7	7 to 9	9 to 11	11 and larger
Recommended Needle Canada/U.K. Size Range	14 to 13	13 to 10	10 to 9	9 to 7	7 to 5	5 to 0	0 and larger

* GUIDELINES ONLY: The above reflect the most commonly used gauges and needle sizes for specific yarn categories.

** Lace weight yarns are usually knitted on larger needles and hooks to create lacy, openwork patterns. Accordingly, a gauge range is difficult to determine. Always follow the gauge stated in your pattern.

CABLES & LACE DISHCLOTH

A quick and super-easy introduction to knitting lace.

Design | Kathy Wesley

Skill Level
EASY

Finished Size
10 inches square

Materials
Worsted weight yarn (140 yds/100g per skein):
  1 skein yellow
Size 8 (5mm) needles or size needed to obtain gauge
Cable needle

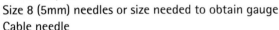
MEDIUM

Gauge
13 sts and 20 rows = 4 inches/10cm in St st
To save time, take time to check gauge.

Special Abbreviation
C8L (Cable 8 Left): Sl next 4 sts onto cn and hold in front of work, k4, k4 from cn.

Pattern Stitch
Cables & Lace

Row 1 (RS): K6, p2, k2tog, yo, k1, p2, k3, p2, k8, p2, k3, p2, k2tog, yo, k1, p2, k6.

Row 2 and all even-numbered rows: K3, [p3, k2] 3 times, p8, [k2, p3] 3 times, k3.

Row 3: K6, p2, k1, yo, ssk, p2, k3, p2, k8, p2, k3, p2, k1, yo, ssk, p2, k6.

Rows 5–8: Rep Rows 1–4.

Rows 9 and 10: Rep Rows 1 and 2.

Row 11: K6, p2, k1, yo, ssk, p2, k3, p2, C8L, p2, k3, p2, k1, yo, ssk, p2, k6.

Row 12: Rep Row 2.

Note
Dishcloth can be worked from chart (see page 28) or from pattern stitch.

Dishcloth

Cast on 44 sts.

Knit 4 rows.

Following Cables & Lace chart or Cables & Lace pat st, [work Rows 1–12] 3 times, then rep Rows 1–9.

Knit 3 rows. Bind off. ∎

Cables & Lace Dishcloth
Sample project was knit with Fantasy
Naturale (100 per cent mercerized
cotton) from Plymouth Yarn Co.

GOSSAMER LACE EVENING WRAP

This wrap is the perfect accent for a formal outfit for that special summer evening out.

Design | Julie Gaddy

Skill Level

EASY

Finished Size

Approx 24 x 68 inches (after blocking and excluding fringe)

Materials

Fingering weight mohair/silk blend yarn
  (225 yds/25g per ball): 5 balls yellow

Size 6 (4mm) circular knitting needle or size
  needed to obtain gauge
Size C/2 (2.75mm) crochet hook

Gauge

21 sts = 4 inches/10cm in pat (blocked)
To save time, take time to check gauge.

Pattern Stitch

Vertical Lace Trellis (multiple of 2 sts + 1)

Rows 1 and 3 (WS): Purl across.

Row 2: K1, *yo, k2tog; rep from * across.

Row 4: *Ssk, yo; rep from * to last st, end k1.

Rep Rows 1–4 for pat.

Notes

To change the size of the wrap, use the following guidelines:

For a longer wrap, add 1 more ball of yarn, which will make the wrap approximately 17 inches longer.

For a wider wrap, cast on an additional 32 stitches (total of 159 stitches) and add 1 more ball of yarn, which will make the wrap approximately 6 inches wider.

For a wrap that is both longer and wider, combine the 2 changes above, which will require 3 additional balls of yarn.

Wrap

Cast on 127 sts.

Rep Rows 1–4 of pat until 1 ball of yarn rem, ending with a WS row.

Bind off all sts kwise.

Wrap will measure approximately 54 inches unblocked.

Finishing

Block wrap.

Fringe

Make triple-knot fringe referring to page 50 as needed. Cut yarn in 24-inch strands; using 2 strands for each knot, fringe each short end of wrap placing knots in every 3rd st.

Trim ends even. ■

Gossamer Lace
Sample project was knit with Douceur et Soie (65 per cent baby mohair/35 per cent silk) from Knit One, Crochet Too.

SURI LACE SCARF

This light and airy mesh scarf is the perfect accessory for late-night strolls in the moonlight.

Design | Lois Young

Skill Level
EASY

Finished Size
9 x 66 inches

Materials
Lace weight yarn (466 yds/50g per ball):
  1 ball purple
Size 7 (4.5mm) needles or size needed to obtain gauge

Gauge
14 sts and 18 rows = 4 inches/10cm in pat
To save time, take time to check gauge.

Pattern Stitch
Lace

Row 1 (RS): Sl 1, k3, *k2tog, yo twice, ssk; rep from * to last 4 sts, end k4.

Row 2: Sl 1, k3 *k1, [p1, k1] in double yo, k1; rep from * to last 4 sts, end k4.

Rep Rows 1 and 2 for pat.

Scarf

Cast on 40 sts.

Top Border
Rows 1–5: Sl 1, k39.

Body

Beg pat

Work Rows 1 and 2 of Lace pat until scarf measures approx 65 inches.

Bottom Border
Rep Rows 1–5 of top border.

Bind off kwise on WS.

Block to measurements by pinning out on flat surface such as rug or bedspread. Mist with water, let dry. Blocking wires can help with this process. ■

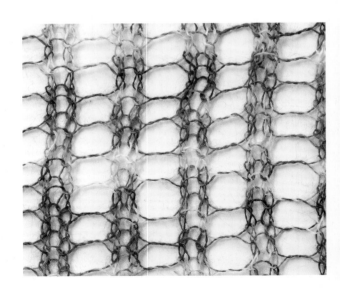

Suri Lace Scarf
Sample project was knit
with Suri (100 per cent suri
alpaca) from Cherry Tree Hill.

CANDLES TRIANGULAR SCARF

This versatile scarf can be worn in a variety of ways. Wear it around your neck for a lovely finishing touch to your outfit or use it to adorn your hair.

Design | Sue Childress

Skill Level

Finished Size
Approx 36 x 17 inches (blocked)

Materials

Worsted weight yarn (85 yds/50g per ball):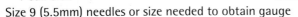
  1 ball blue

4 MEDIUM

Size 9 (5.5mm) needles or size needed to obtain gauge

Gauge

16 sts = 4 inches/10cm (before blocking)
To save time, take time to check gauge.

Scarf

Cast on 3 sts.

Row 1 (RS): Knit.

Row 2: Purl.

Row 3: [K1, yo] twice, k1—5 sts.

Row 4 and all even-numbered rows until Row 80: Purl.

Row 5: K1, yo, k3, yo, k1—7 sts.

Row 7: K1, yo, knit to last st, yo, k1.

Row 8: Rep Row 4.

Rows 9–14: [Rep Rows 7 and 8] 3 times.

Row 15: K1, yo, k4, k2tog, yo, k1, yo, ssk, k4, yo, k1—17 sts.

Row 17: K1, yo, k4, k2tog, yo, k3, yo, ssk, k4, yo, k1—19 sts.

Row 19: K1, yo, k4, [k2tog, yo] twice, k1, [yo, ssk] twice, k4, yo, k1—21 sts.

Row 21: K1, yo, k4, [k2tog, yo] twice, k3, [yo, ssk] twice, k4, yo, k1—23 sts.

Row 23: K1, yo, k4, [k2tog, yo] 3 times, k1, [yo, ssk] 3 times, k4, yo, k1—25 sts.

Rows 25–32: [Rep Rows 7 and 8] 4 times—33 sts.

Row 33: K1, yo, k6, k2tog, yo, k1, yo, ssk, k9, k2tog, yo, k1, yo, ssk, k6, yo, k1—35 sts.

Row 35: K1, yo, k6, k2tog, yo, k3, yo, ssk, k7, k2tog, yo, k3, yo, ssk, k6, yo, k1—37 sts.

Row 37: K1, yo, k6, [k2tog, yo] twice, k1, [yo, ssk] twice, k5, [k2tog, yo] twice, k1, [yo, ssk] twice, k6, yo, k1—39 sts.

Row 39: K1, yo, k6, [k2tog, yo] twice, k3, [yo, ssk] twice, k3, [k2tog, yo] twice, k3, [yo, ssk] twice, k6, yo, k1—41 sts.

Row 41: K1, yo, k6, [k2tog, yo] 3 times, k1, [yo, ssk] 3 times, k1, [k2tog, yo] 3 times, k1, [yo, ssk] 3 times, k6, yo, k1—43 sts.

Rows 43–52: [Rep Rows 7 and 8] 3 times—53 sts.

Row 53: K1, yo, k9, [k2tog, yo, k1, yo, ssk, k9] 3 times, yo, k1—55 sts.

Candles Triangular Scarf
Sample project was knit with Katia
Idea (50 per cent cotton, 35 per
cent rayon, 15 per cent linen) from
Knitting Fever.

Row 55: K1, yo, k9, [k2tog, yo, k3, yo, ssk, k7] 3 times, k2, yo, k1—57 sts.

Row 57: K1, yo, k9, [(k2tog, yo) twice, k1, (yo, ssk) twice, k5] 3 times, k4, yo, k1—59 sts.

Row 59: K1, yo, k9, [(k2tog, yo) twice, k3, (yo, ssk) twice, k3] 3 times, k6, yo, k1—61 sts.

Row 61: K1, yo, k9, [(k2tog, yo) 3 times, k1, (yo, ssk) 3 times, k1] 3 times, k8, yo, k1—63 sts.

Rows 63–78: [Rep Rows 7 and 8] 3 times—79 sts.

Row 79: K1, yo, knit to last st, yo, k1—81 sts.

Row 80 (WS): P2, *p2tog, yo, rep from * to last 3 sts, yo, p3.

Rows 81–86: [Rep Rows 7 and 8] 3 times.

Rows 87 and 88: Rep Rows 79 and 80.

Row 89: [K1, yo] twice, knit to last 2 sts, [yo, k1] twice.

Row 90: Purl.

Rows 91–100: [Rep Rows 89 and 90] 5 times.

Bind off all sts in purl.

Wet-block for best results. ■

BLUEBERRY LACE

Hourglass cables form a lovely openwork pattern on a lacy afghan.

Design | Sue Childress

Skill Level
EASY

Finished Size
Approx 45 x 54 inches

Materials
Chunky weight yarn (143 yds/100g per ball):
   9 balls blue heather
Size 11 (8mm) 30-inch circular needle or size
   needed to obtain gauge
Stitch markers

5 BULKY

Gauge
10 sts and 8 rows = 4 inches/10cm in pat
To save time, take time to check gauge.

Pattern Stitches
Border

Row 1 (RS): K2, *p3, k2; rep from * across.

Rows 2 and 4: Purl.

Row 3: *P3, k2; rep from * to last 2 sts, p2.

Row 5: Purl.

Row 6: Rep Row 3.

Row 7: Purl.

Hourglass Cables

Row 1 (RS): [K2, p3] twice, k3; slip marker, k5, *p1, k5; rep from * to marker; slip marker, k3, [p3, k2] twice.

Row 2: P12, k1, slip marker, *p5, k1; rep from * to 5 sts before marker, p5; slip marker, k1, p12.

Row 3: [P3, k2] twice, p2, k1; slip marker, yo, ssk, p1, k2tog, yo, *k1, yo, ssk, p1, k2tog, yo; rep from * to marker; slip marker, k1, [p3, k2] twice, p2.

Row 4: P12, k1; slip marker, *p2, k1, p3; rep from * to 5 sts before marker, p2, k1, p2; slip marker, k1, p12.

Row 5: [K2, p3] twice, k3; slip marker, k2, p1, k2, *k3, p1, k2; rep from * to marker, k1; slip marker, k3, [p3, k2] twice.

Row 6: Rep Row 4.

Row 7: [P3, k2] twice, p2, k1; slip marker, k2tog, yo, k1, yo, ssk, *p1, k2tog, yo, k1, yo, ssk; rep from * to marker, slip marker, k1, [p3, k2] twice, p2.

Row 8: Rep Row 2.

Rep Rows 1–8 for pat.

Note
Circular needle is used to accommodate large number of stitches. Do not join; work in rows.

Afghan

Cast on 137 sts.

Knit 1 row.

Work 7 rows of Border pat.

Inc row: Purl in front and back of first st, purl 11, place marker, purl to last 12 sts, place marker, purl to last st, purl in front and back of last st—139 sts.

[Work Rows 1–8 of Hourglass Cables pat] 22 times; rep Rows 1–7.

Dec row: P2tog, p10, k1, *p5, k1; rep from * to last 12 sts, p10, p2tog—137 sts.

Work Rows 1–7 of Border pat.

Purl 1 row; knit 1 row.

Bind off. ■

Blueberry Lace
Sample project was knit with Encore Chunky (75 per cent acrylic/25 per cent wool) from Plymouth Yarn Co.

IRISH NET VALANCE

*Enhance your favourite view
with an Irish net lace layer.*

Design | Darlene Dale

Skill Level
EASY

Finished Size
Approx 18 x 60 inches

Materials
DK weight yarn (251 yds/85g per ball):
   4 balls ecru
Size 7 (4.5mm) needles or size needed to obtain
   gauge

Gauge
20 sts and 24 rows = 4 inches/10cm in pat; 20 sts and
   32 rows = 4 inches/10cm in garter st
To save time, take time to check gauge.

Pattern Stitch
Irish Net (multiple of 3 sts)

Row 1 (RS): K2, *yo, sl 1, k2, psso 2 knit sts; rep from * to
last st, end k1.

Row 2: Purl across.

Row 3: K1, *sl 1, k2, psso 2 knit sts, yo; rep from * to last
2 sts, end k2.

Row 4: Purl across.

Rep Rows 1–4 for pat.

Notes
Valance is knitted sideways.

Slip all stitches knitwise.

Valance
Cast on 81 sts, knit 3 rows.

Work first and last 3 sts in garter st throughout, work
pat on 75 sts until valance measures approx 59½ inches,
ending with a RS row.

Work 3 rows garter st. Bind off all sts.

Tabs
Make 8

Cast on 10 sts and work in garter st until tab measures
4 inches. Bind off.

Assembly
Block to measurements.

At each end, sew 1 end of tab on RS over 3 rows of garter
st; sew other end to top edge of garter st on WS. Sew rem
tabs evenly spaced across. ■

Irish Net Valance
Sample project was knit with Spa
(75 per cent microdenier acrylic/
25 per cent rayon from bamboo)
from NaturallyCaron.com.

MAKE MINE COLOURFUL THROW

Openwork and ribs give a slightly different appearance to each side of this reversible throw.

Design | Kennita Tully

Skill Level

EASY

Finished Size

Approx 48 x 58 inches

Materials

Super chunky weight yarn (59 yds/100g per ball):
  15 balls pastel multi
Size 15 (10mm) 29-inch circular needle or size
  needed to obtain gauge

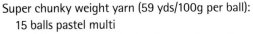

SUPER BULKY

Gauge

9 sts and 9 rows = 4 inches/10cm in Double Lace Rib pat
To save time, take time to check gauge.

Pattern Stitch

Double Lace Rib

Row 1 (RS): K3, *p1, yo, k2tog-tbl, p1, k2; rep from * to last st, k1.

Rows 2 and 4: P3, *k1, p2; rep from * to last st, p1.

Row 3: K3, *p1, k2tog, yo, p1, k2; rep from * to last st, k1.

Rep Rows 1–4 for pat.

Note

Circular needle is used to accommodate large number of stitches. Do not join; work in rows.

Throw

Cast on 106 sts.

Beg with Row 2 of pat, work even in pat for approx 58 inches, ending with Row 1.

Bind off in pat. ■

Make Mine Colourful Throw
Sample project was knit with Yukon
Print (35 per cent wool/35 per cent
mohair/30 per cent acrylic) from
Plymouth Yarn Co.

EASY LACE COWL

Whip up this easy cowl for yourself or a lucky friend.

Design | Kim Guzman

Skill Level
EASY

Size
One size fits most

Finished Measurement
Approx 5 x 46 inches (after blocking)

Materials
Sport weight yarn (168 yds/50g per ball):
  1 ball purple
Size 4 (3.5mm) 24-inch circular needle or size
  needed to obtain gauge
Stitch marker

2 FINE

Gauge
22 sts and 36 rnds = 4 inches/10cm in St st (blocked)
Gauge is not critical to this project.

Pattern Stitches
Rib (multiple of 7 sts)

Rnd 1: P1, *k5, p2; rep from * to last 6 sts, k5, p1.

Rep Rnd 1 for pat.

Lace (multiple of 7 sts)

Rnd 1: P1, *k2tog, yo, k1, yo, ssk, p2; rep from * to last 6 sts, k2tog, yo, k1, yo, ssk, p1.

Rnds 2–4: P1, *k5, p2; rep from * to last 6 sts, k5, p1.

Rep Rnds 1–4 for pat.

Note
This easy lace cowl is worked in the round with a simple 4-round repeat, with only 1 of those rounds including typical lace stitches. The rest is worked on an easy, more familiar 5 x 2 rib.

Cowl
Cast on 203 sts. Place marker for beg of rnd and join without twisting.

Work in Rib pat until cowl measures 1 inch from cast-on edge.

Change to Lace pat and work until cowl measures 7 inches from cast-on edge, ending with Rnd 1 of pat.

Change to Rib pat and work until cowl measures 8 inches from cast-on edge.

Bind off loosely in pat.

Finishing
Immerse completely in water. Gently squeeze out water, and then roll in dry towel to remove excess water. Lie flat, stretching widthwise to block out the ribbing. (This causes the height to shorten.) Allow to dry completely. ■

Easy Lace Cowl

Sample project was knit with Rayon
Petalspun (100 per cent rayon) from
Pisgah Yarn & Dyeing Co.

EVENING OUT

What a way to show off your new knitting skills—a great wrap for a perfect evening on the town.

Design | George Shaheen

Skill Level
EASY

Sizes
Woman's small/medium (large/extra-large) Instructions are given for smallest size, with larger size in parentheses. When only one number is given, it applies to both sizes.

Finished Measurements
Approx 38 x 19 (46 x 20) inches (excluding fringe)

Materials
Worsted weight yarn (115 yds/50g per ball):
  6 balls bronze

Size 11 (8mm) 36-inch circular needle
Size 15 (10mm) 36-inch circular needle or size needed to obtain gauge
Size H/8 (5mm) crochet hook
¾-inch black button
Sewing needle and matching thread

Gauge
14 sts = 4 inches/10cm in pat with larger needle (before blocking)
To save time, take time to check gauge.

Notes
Circular needle is used to accommodate large number of stitches. Do not join; work in rows.

When measuring, be sure piece is flat and not stretched as this pattern tends to grow vertically and shrink horizontally.

Poncho

Body
With larger needle, cast on 146 (178) sts.

Row 1 (WS): P1, *p3tog, work (k1, p1, k1) in next st; rep from * to last st, p1.

Rows 2 and 4: Purl.

Row 3: P1, *work (k1, p1, k1) in next st, p3tog; rep from * to last st, p1.

Rep Rows 1–4 until piece measures approx 16 (17) inches, ending with Row 2.

Change to smaller needles.

Shape neck
Row 1: P1, [work (k1, p1, k1) in next st, p3tog] 9 (10) times, *work (k1, p1, k1) in next st, p3tog, p1, p3tog, work (k1, p1, k1) in next st, p3tog; rep from * 5 (7) times, [work (k1, p1, k1) in next st, p3tog] 9 (10) times, p1—134 (162) sts.

Rows 2, 4 and 6: Purl.

Row 3: P39 (43), *p2tog, p3; rep from * 11 (15) times, p35 (39)—122 (146) sts.

Row 5: P37 (41), *p2tog, p2; rep from * 11 (15) times, p37 (41)—110 (130) sts.

Evening Out
Sample project was knit with
Glitterspun Yarn (60 per cent
acrylic/27 per cent cupro/13 per cent
polyester) from Lion Brand Yarn.

Bind off as follows: P38 (42), *p2tog, p1, rep from * 11 (15) times, p36 (40).

Block piece to measure 38 x 19 inches (46 x 20 inches).

Fringe

Make triple-knot fringe referring to Fringe side bar as needed. Cut strands of yarn, each 18 inches long; use 4 strands for each knot.

Tie 1 knot in every 4th st across bottom edge and every 5th row across side edges. Tie 2 knots in each corner.

When tying the 3rd row of knots, do not tie a knot in the first or last strand of the fringe.

Assembly

Lay piece flat with WS facing. Referring to photo, fold right-hand edge to meet left-hand edge. Sew upper left back corner over upper left front corner, overlapping 2 (2½) inches at neck edge and having tip of back corner 1 inch from side edge.

Sew button through all layers of corner closure. ∎

Fringe

Cut a piece of cardboard half as long as specified in instructions for length of strands plus ½ inch for trimming. Wind yarn loosely and evenly around cardboard. When cardboard is filled, cut yarn across one end. Do this several times, then begin fringing. Wind additional strands as necessary.

Single-Knot Fringe

Hold specified number of strands for one knot together, fold in half. Hold project to be fringed with right side facing you. Use crochet hook to draw folded end through space or stitch indicated from right to wrong side.

Pull loose ends through folded section. Draw knot up firmly. Space knots as indicated in pattern instructions.

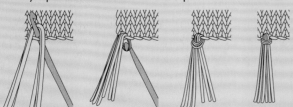

Single-Knot Fringe

Double-Knot Fringe

With RS facing, working from left to right, take half the strands of 1 knot and half the strands in the knot next to it, and tie group tog in an overhand knot.

Double-Knot Fringe

Triple-Knot Fringe

Tie another row of knots, using alternate strands of yarn from previous row.

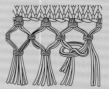

Triple-Knot Fringe

SIMPLE LACE TOP

Ribbing gently defines the waistline of this soft lace shell.

Design | Cecily Glowik MacDonald

Skill Level

EASY

Sizes

Woman's small (medium, large, extra-large, 2X-large) Instructions are given for smallest size, with larger sizes in parentheses. When only one number is given, it applies to all sizes.

Finished Measurements

Chest: 33½ (38, 42, 46½, 51) inches
Length: 22 inches

Materials

Worsted weight yarn (77 yds/50g per ball):
   8 (9, 10, 11, 12) balls blue
Size 5 (3.75mm) needles
Size 6 (4mm) needles or size needed to obtain gauge
Stitch markers
8 (⅝-inch) buttons

Gauge

22 sts and 26 rows = 4 inches/10cm in Lace Rib pat with
   larger needles (blocked)
To save time, take time to check gauge.

Pattern Stitches

Lace Rib (multiple of 6 sts + 2)

Row 1 (RS): K2, *p1, yo, k2tog, p1, k2; rep from * across.

Row 2: P2, *k1, p2; rep from * across.

Row 3: K2, *p1, k2tog, yo, p1, k2; rep from * across.

Row 4: Rep Row 2.

Rep Rows 1–4 for pat.

P4, K2 Rib (multiple of 6 sts + 2)

RS rows: K2, *p4, k2; rep from * across.

WS rows: Knit the knit sts and purl the purl sts as they face you.

Rep these 2 rows for pat.

Top

Back/Front
Make 2

With larger needles, cast on 92 (104, 116, 128, 140) sts. Work Lace Rib pat until piece measures 3½ inches from beg, ending with a WS row.

Change to smaller needles and work P4, K2 Rib until piece measures 6½ inches from beg, ending with a WS row.

Change to larger needles and work in Lace Rib pat until piece measures 14 (14, 13, 13, 12) inches from beg. Mark each end of row.

Beg on next row, sl first st of every row and work in pat until piece measures 22 inches from beg, ending with a RS row.

Next row (WS): Bind off all sts in pat.

Assembly
Block pieces to required measurements. Sew side seams from bottom to marked row—14 (14, 13, 13, 13) inches.

Shoulders
Beg at outer edges, sew bound-off edges tog for 4 (5, 5½, 6½, 7½) inches.

Referring to photo, sew 4 buttons evenly across each shoulder seam. ■

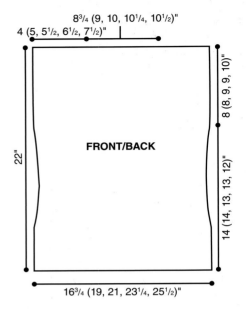

8¾ (9, 10, 10¼, 10½)"
4 (5, 5½, 6½, 7½)"

8 (8, 9, 9, 10)"

FRONT/BACK

22"

14 (14, 13, 13, 12)"

16¾ (19, 21, 23¼, 25½)"

Simple Lace Top
Sample project was knit with
Bam Boo (100 per cent bamboo)
from Classic Elite Yarns.

SNOW BUNNY CARDIGAN

Keep her cozy in this darling hooded cardigan. It's easier than it looks!

Design | Celeste Pinheiro

Skill Level

Sizes

Child's 2 (4, 6) Instructions are given for smallest size, with larger sizes in parentheses. When only one number is given, it applies to all sizes.

Finished Measurements

Chest: 25 (30, 35) inches
Length: 13 (15, 17) inches, excluding hood

Materials

Chunky weight yarn (143 yds/100g per ball): 3 (4, 4) balls blue (MC)
Super chunky weight yarn (52 yds/50g per ball): 2 balls blue (CC)
Size 10 (6mm) needles or size needed to obtain gauge
Size J/10 (6mm) crochet hook
4-inch piece cardboard

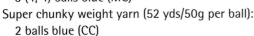

Gauge

16 sts = 5 inches/12.5cm in pat
To save time, take time to check gauge.

Special Abbreviation

MB (make bobble): [K1, p1, k1, p1, k1] into next st, [turn, p5; turn, k5] twice, pass 4 sts over last st—1 st rem.

Pattern Stitch

Diamond Lace (multiple of 8 sts + 3)

Row 1 (RS): K1, *k2, k2tog, yo, k1, yo, ssk, k1; rep from * to last 2 sts, end k2.

Rows 2, 4, 6, 8 and 10: K1, purl to last st, end k1.

Row 3: K1, *k1, k2tog, yo, k3, yo, ssk; rep from * to last 2 sts, end k2.

Row 5 (on first rep): K1, k2tog, *yo, k2, MB, k2, yo, sl 1, k2tog, psso; rep from * to last 8 sts, end yo, k2, MB, k2, yo, ssk, k1.

Row 5 (all rem reps): K1, k2tog, *yo, k5, yo, sl 1, k2tog, psso; rep from * to last 8 sts, end yo, k5, yo, ssk, k1.

Row 7: K1, *k1, yo, ssk, k3, k2tog, yo; rep from * to last 2 sts, end k2.

Row 9: K1, *k2, yo, ssk, k1, k2tog, yo, k1; rep from * to last 2 sts, end k2.

Row 11: K1, *k3, yo, sl 1, k2tog, psso, yo, k2; rep from * to last 2 sts, end k2.

Row 12: K1, purl to last st, end k1.

Rep Rows 1–12 for pat, omitting bobbles in Row 5 after first time.

Snow Bunny Cardigan
Sample project was knit with Encore
Chunky (75 per cent acrylic/25 per
cent wool) and Coloura (65 per cent nylon/35 per
cent polyester) from Plymouth Yarn Co.

Notes

Number of stitches cast on includes 1 edge stitch at each side (included in pattern); knit these stitches every row, work shaping inside these stitches.

When working shaping, if there aren't enough stitches to work an increase and its matching decrease, work stitches in stockinette stitch.

Cardigan

Back

With MC, cast on 43 (51, 59) sts. Knit 5 rows, ending with a WS row.

Beg Diamond Lace pat and work even until back measures 7 (8½, 10) inches from beg, ending with a WS row.

Shape armholes

Maintaining pat, bind off 4 sts at beg of next 2 rows—35 (43, 51) sts.

Work even until back measures 12½ (14½, 16½) inches from beg, ending with a WS row.

Shape neck

Work 11 (14, 17) sts, attach 2nd ball of yarn, bind off centre 13 (15, 17) sts, work to end.

Working both sides at once, dec 1 st at each neck edge once, then work even on rem 10 (13, 16) sts until back measures 13 (15, 17) inches from beg. Bind off rem sts.

Left Front

With MC, cast on 19 (27, 27) sts. Knit 5 rows, ending with a WS row.

Beg Diamond Lace pat and work even until front measures 7 (8½, 10) inches from beg, ending with a WS row.

Shape armhole

Maintaining pat, bind off 4 sts at beg of next row—15 (23, 23) sts.

Work even until front measures 11 (13, 15) inches from beg, ending with a RS row.

Shape neck

Bind off 5 (10, 7) sts at neck edge—10 (13, 16) sts.

Work even in pat until front measures 13 (15, 17) inches from beg, bind off rem sts.

Right Front

Work as for left front to underarm, ending with a RS row.

Shape armhole

Maintaining pat, bind off 4 sts at beg of next row—15 (23, 23) sts.

Work even until front measures 11 (13, 15) inches from beg, ending with a WS row.

Shape neck

Bind off 5 (10, 7) sts at neck edge—10 (13, 16) sts.

Work even in pat until front measures 13 (15, 17) inches from beg, bind off rem sts.

Sleeves
Make 2

With CC, cast on 27 sts. Knit 5 rows, ending with a WS row.

Change to MC, beg Diamond Lace pat, and *at the same time*, working inside edge sts, inc 1 st at each side [every 4th row] 8 (10, 12) times, working added sts into pat—43, (47, 51) sts.

Work even in pat until sleeve measures 11 (12, 13) inches from beg. Bind off all sts.

Assembly

Sew shoulder seams. Sew sleeves into armholes, and then sew side and sleeve seams.

Hood

With MC, RS facing, pick up and knit 43 (51, 51) sts evenly around neck.

Beg Diamond Lace pat (do not work bobbles), work even until hood measures 8 (8½, 9) inches from beg, ending with a WS row.

Shape hood

Row 1 (RS): Maintaining pat throughout, work 20 (24, 24) sts, sl 1, k2tog, psso, work to end.

Rows 2, 4, 6 and 8: Purl across.

Row 3: Work 19 (23, 23) sts, sl 1, k2tog, psso, work to end.

Row 5: Work 18 (22, 22) sts, sl 1, k2tog, psso, work to end.

Row 7: Work 17 (21, 21) sts, sl 1, k2tog, psso, work to end.

Row 9: Work 16 (20, 20) sts, sl 1, k2tog, psso, work to end.

Row 10: Purl across.

Bind off rem 33 (41, 41) sts.

Fold hood, sew seam.

Front Band

Beg at bottom of right front with CC, RS facing, pick up and knit 196 (202, 208) sts evenly around front edges and hood. Knit 5 rows, bind off all sts.

Ties
Make 2

With MC doubled, crochet a 16 (17, 18)-inch chain (see page 25). Fasten off, leaving a long tail.

Pompoms
Make 2

With CC, wrap strand around a 4-inch piece of cardboard 40 times. Using tails of ties, tie very firmly around middle of wraps, cut loops. Sew ties to front neck edges. ∎

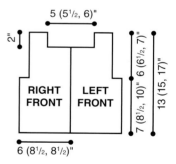

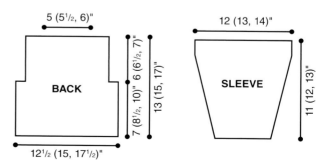

BUTTERCUP BABY SET

Welcome the newborn with these easy-knit beauties.

Designs | Sherry Graziano

Skill Level
EASY

Size
Newborn

Finished Measurements
Sweater Chest: 22 inches
Sweater Length: Approx 10 inches
Bonnet: Approx 12 inches around front
Booties: Approx 4 inches long

Materials
Worsted weight yarn (200 yds/100g per ball):
   2 balls yellow
Size 8 (5mm) needles or size needed to obtain gauge
Size 10 (6mm) needles or size needed to obtain gauge
Stitch markers
Stitch holders
Approx 2½ yds ⅜-inch-wide ribbon

4
MEDIUM

Gauge
15 sts and 20 rows = 4 inches/10cm in St st with larger
  needles for sweater and bonnet
10 sts = 2 inches/5cm in garter st with smaller needles
  for booties
To save time, take time to check gauge.

Special Abbreviation
Increase 1 (inc 1): Knit into front and back of same st
(1 st inc).

Note
Yarn and ribbon amounts given are sufficient to complete set.

Sweater

Body
Note: Keep 3 sts at each edge of body in garter st throughout.

Beg at top with larger needles, cast on 35 sts.

Row 1 (RS): Knit across.

Row 2: Purl across.

Row 3 (eyelet row): K3, place marker, *k2tog, yo; rep from * to last 4 sts, end k1, place marker, k3.

Row 4 and all rem even-numbered rows: K3, purl to last 3 sts, end k3.

Row 5: K3, inc 1, *k1, inc 1; rep from * to last 3 sts, end k3—50 sts.

Row 7: K3, *k2tog, yo; rep from * to last 3 sts, end k3.

Row 9: K3, *k2, inc 1; rep from * to last 5 sts, end k5—64 sts.

Row 11: Rep Row 7.

Row 13: K5, *inc 1, k3; rep from * to last 3 sts, end k3—78 sts.

Buttercup Baby Set
Sample project was knit with Encore
Worsted (75 per cent acrylic/25 per
cent wool) from Plymouth Yarn Co.

Row 15: Rep Row 7.

Row 17: K5, *inc 1, k4; rep from * to last 3 sts, end k3—92 sts.

Row 19: Rep Row 7.

Row 21: K5, *inc 1, k5; rep from * to last 3 sts, end k3—106 sts.

Row 23: Rep Row 7.

Row 25: Place markers as follows: K3, slip marker, k14, inc 1, place marker, inc 1, k15, inc 1, place marker, inc 1, k34, inc 1, place marker, inc 1, k15, inc 1, place marker, inc 1, k14, slip marker, k3—114 sts.

Row 26: Knit first 3 and last 3 sts, slip all markers and purl rem sts.

Row 27: Inc 1 st on each side of markers except at front borders—122 sts.

Row 28: Rep Row 26.

Rows 29 and 30: Rep Rows 27 and 28.

Row 31 (dividing row): Knit to first sleeve marker (21 left front sts), sl next 23 sts to a holder for sleeve, knit next 42 sts (back), sl next 23 sts to a holder for 2nd sleeve, knit rem 21 sts for right front—84 sts on needle for body.

Work in St st until body measures 5 inches from underarm, maintaining garter st borders on each side, and ending with a WS row.

Picot row: *K2tog, yo; rep from * to last 2 sts, end k2tog—83 sts.

Beg with a purl row, work 3 rows in St st. Bind off all sts.

Sleeve

Sl 23 sleeve sts to needle, join yarn and work in St st until sleeve measures 4 inches from underarm.

Change to smaller needles.

Next row: K1, p1, *k2tog, p1, k1, p1; rep from * to last st, end k1—19 sts.

Next row: P1, *k1, p1; rep from * across.

Next row: K1, *p1, k1; rep from * across.

Rep last 2 rows for 1½ inches. Bind off in pat.

Rep for 2nd sleeve.

Assembly

Sew sleeve seams.

Turn up bottom hem so eyelet row forms a scalloped edge; sew in place. Weave ribbon through top eyelet row for tie.

Bonnet

With larger needles, cast on 15 sts and work in St st for 3½ inches, ending with a WS row.

Using cable cast-on (see page 27), cast on 12 sts at beg of next 2 rows—39 sts.

Work 2 rows in St st.

Eyelet pat

Row 1: *K2tog, yo; rep from * to last st, end k1.

Rows 2–4: Work 3 rows in St st.

Rows 5–12: Rep Rows 1–4.

Rows 13 and 14: Work in St st.

Row 15: Rep Row 1.

Rows 16–18: Work in St st.

Bind off all sts.

Sew seams; turn up front hem so eyelet row forms a scalloped edge, sew in place. Sew a ribbon on each front corner for tie.

Booties

Bootie
Make 2

With smaller needles, cast on 35 sts.

Row 1: K1, inc 1, k14, inc 1, place marker, k1, place marker, inc 1, k14, inc 1, k1—39 sts.

Row 2: Knit across, slip markers.

Row 3: K1, inc 1, knit to 1 st before marker, inc 1, slip marker, k1, slip marker, inc 1, knit to last 2 sts, end inc 1, k1—43 sts.

Row 4: Rep Row 2.

Row 5: Rep Row 3—47 sts.

Rows 6–11: Work in garter st, removing markers.

Shape instep
Row 12 (WS): K20, p7, p3tog, turn.

Row 13: Sl 1, k7, sl 1, k2tog, psso, turn.

Row 14: Sl 1, p7, p3tog, turn.

Rows 15–20: [Rep last 2 rows] 3 times.

Row 21: Rep Row 13 once, knit to end of needle—27 sts rem; 10 sts on each side and 7 sts in centre.

Knit 1 row even.

Eyelet row: *K2tog, yo; rep from * to last st, end k1.

Work in k1, p1 rib for 2½ inches. Bind off all sts in pat.

Sew seam from toe to top of cuff. Weave ribbon through eyelet row for ties. ∎

NATURAL BEAUTY FOR BABY

Welcome Baby to the world with a wonderfully patterned top-down, raglan-sleeve sweater and matching hat.

Designs | Nazanin S. Fard

Skill Level

EASY

Sizes
Newborn (6, 12 months) Instructions are given for smallest size, with larger sizes in parentheses. When only one number is given, it applies to all sizes.

Finished Measurements
Chest: 19¼ (23¼, 25¼) inches
Length: 9¾ (11½, 12) inches
Hat circumference: 15 inches

Materials
Worsted weight yarn (216 yds/100g per ball):
  2 (2, 3) balls ecru
Size 6 (4mm) double-point and 29-inch circular
  needles or size needed to obtain gauge
Size F/5 (3.75mm) crochet hook
Stitch markers
4 (⁷⁄₁₆-inch) buttons

Gauge
20 sts and 28 rows = 4 inches/10cm in St st
To save time, take time to check gauge.

Special Abbreviations
Place marker (pm): Place marker on needle.

Slip marker (sm): Slip marker from LH needle to RH needle.

Make 1 (M1): Inc by making backward loop on RH needle.

Knit in front and back (kfb): Knit in front and then in back of next st.

Slip, knit 2 together, pass (sk2p): Slip next st, k2tog, pass slipped st over k2tog and off needle to dec 2 sts.

Pattern Stitch
Lace (multiple of 5 sts)

Row/Rnd 1: *K2tog, k3, yo; rep from * to end.

Row 2 and all even-numbered rows: Purl across.

Rnd 2 and all even-numbered rnds: Knit around.

Row/Rnd 3: *K2tog, k2, yo, k1; rep from * to end.

Row/Rnd 5: *K2tog, k1, yo, k2; rep from * to end.

Row/Rnd 7: *K2tog, yo, k3; rep from * to end.

Row/Rnd 9: *Yo, k3, ssk; rep from * to end.

Row/Rnd 11: *K1, yo, k2, ssk; rep from * to end.

Row/Rnd 13: *K2, yo, k1, ssk; rep from * to end.

Row/Rnd 15: *K3, yo, ssk; rep from * to end.

Row 16: Purl across.

Rnd 16: Knit around.

Rep Rows/Rnds 1–16 for pat.

Natural Beauty for Baby
Sample project was knit with Berella 4 (100 per cent acrylic) from Bernat.

sts, pm, 1 raglan seam st, pm, 16 (20, 20) back sts, pm, 1 raglan seam st, pm, 6 (5, 7) sleeve sts, pm, 1 raglan seam st, pm, 1 front st.

Row 2: Purl across.

Row 3 (inc row): *Knit to marker, M1, sm, k1, sm, M1; rep from * 3 times more, knit to end—42 (44, 48) sts.

Note: At the same time, *make buttonhole in right front garter border on first (2nd, 2nd), on 4th (5th, 5th), and then on 7th (8th, 8th) inc row as follows: K1, yo, k2tog.*

Row 4: Purl across.

Row 5 (RS): Kfb, *knit to marker, M1, sm, k1, sm, M1; rep from * 3 times more, knit to last st, kfb—52 (54, 58) sts.

Row 6: Purl across.

Rep [Rows 5 and 6] 2 (3, 4) times—72 (84, 98) sts.

Next row (RS): Cast on 5 (6, 7) sts, *knit to marker, M1, sm, k1, sm, M1; rep from * 3 times more, knit to end, cast on 5 (6, 7) sts—90 (104, 120) sts.

Next row (WS): K3, purl to last 3 sts, k3.

Rep [rows 3 and 4] 6 (7, 8) more times, then rep row 3—146 (168, 192) sts.

Body

Next row (WS): Removing markers, k3, p19 (23, 27), slip next 30 (33, 39) sleeve sts to waste yarn, cable cast-on (see page 27) 5 (7, 6) underarm sts, p42 (50, 54), slip next 30 (33, 39) sleeve sts to waste yarn, cable cast on 5 (7, 6) underarm sts, p19 (23, 27), k3—96 (116, 126) sts.

Next row (RS): K3, work Row 1 of Lace pat to last 3 sts, k3.

Notes

The sweater is worked from the raglan yoke down. The sleeves are worked in the round from the yoke down.

The yoke and lower body are worked back and forth on a circular needle.

A chart is included for those preferring to work Lace pattern from a chart. When working in rounds, all rows are worked from right to left.

Sweater

Yoke

Cast on 34 (36, 40) sts. Do not join; work back and forth in rows.

Row 1 (set-up row): Knit across, placing markers as follows: 1 front st, pm, 1 raglan seam st, pm, 6 (5, 7) sleeve

Maintaining 3-st garter border, work even in Lace pat until body measures approx 5¾ (7, 7) inches, or ½ inch less than desired length from underarm, ending with Row 8 or 16 of pat.

Knit 6 rows. Bind off all sts loosely.

Sleeves

Pick up and knit 3 sts from underarm, pm for beg of rnd, pick up and knit 2 (4, 3) underarm sts, slip sts from waste yarn to dpns and knit to end of rnd—35 (40, 45 sts).

Continue working Lace pat in rnds until sleeve measures approx 5¾ (7, 8) inches, or ½ inch less than desired length from underarm, ending with Rnd 8 or 16 of pat.

[Knit 1 rnd, purl 1 rnd] 3 times.

Bind off all sts loosely.

Rep for other sleeve.

Neck Edging

With RS facing, pick up and knit 59 (65, 73) sts around neck edge.

Row 1 (WS): P1, *k1, p1, rep from * across.

Row 2: Knit the knit sts and purl the purl sts across.

Row 3: Work in rib to last 3 sts, p2tog, yo, p1.

Rows 4 and 5: Work in established rib pat.

Bind off very loosely in rib.

Front Edging

Note: If not familiar with single crochet (sc) and reverse single crochet (reverse sc), refer to Crochet Basics on page 25.

Row 1: With RS facing and crochet hook, work 1 row of sc along right front. Do not turn.

Row 2 (RS): Work reverse sc along the edge. Fasten off.

Rep on left front.

Block to finished measurements.

Sew buttons to left front opposite buttonholes.

Hat

With 2 dpns, cast on 3 sts and work I-cord as follows: *K3, do not turn, slip sts back to LH needle; rep from * for 15 rows.

Beg working in rnds.

Rnd 1: Kfb of each st. Place 2 sts on each of 3 needles, pm for beg of rnd and join without twisting—6 sts.

Rnd 2 and all even-numbered rnds: Knit around.

Rnd 3: *K1, yo, k1; rep from * around—9 sts.

Rnd 5: *[K1, yo] twice, k1; rep from * around—15 sts.

Rnd 7: *K1, yo, k3, yo, k1; rep from * around—21 sts.

Rnd 9: *K1, yo, k5, yo, k1; rep from * around— 27 sts.

Rnd 11: *Yo, k1, yo, ssk, k3, k2tog, yo, k1; rep from * around—30 sts.

Rnd 13: *K1, yo, k2, yo, ssk, k1, k2tog, yo, k2, yo; rep from * around—36 sts.

Rnd 15: *K2, yo, k3, yo, sk2p, yo, k3, yo, k1; rep from * around—42 sts.

Rnd 17: *K3, yo, k9, yo, k2; rep from * around—48 sts.

Rnd 19: *K4, yo, k9, yo, k3; rep from * around—54 sts.

Rnd 21: *K5, yo, k9, yo, k4; rep from * around—60 sts.

Purl 2 rnds.

Work [Rnds 1–16 of Lace pat] twice.

[Knit 1 rnd, purl 1 rnd] 3 times.

Bind off all sts loosely. Block. ■

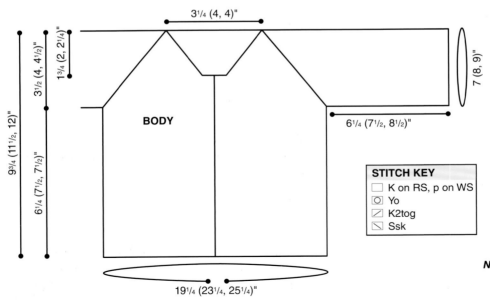

STITCH KEY
☐ K on RS, p on WS
⊙ Yo
╱ K2tog
╲ Ssk

LACE CHART

*Note: Sleeve is worked in rnds.
Rep is worked from right
to left on all rnds.*

SPRINGTIME BERET

Keep your shining mane tamed with a soft little beret of lace!

Design | Cecily Glowik MacDonald

Skill Level

INTERMEDIATE

Size
Woman's, one size fits most

Finished Measurement
Circumference: Approx 20 inches (slightly stretched)

Materials
Bulky weight yarn (109 yds/100g per hank):
   1 hank ecru

5 BULKY

Size 8 (5mm) 16-inch circular needle
Size 10 (6mm) 16-inch circular and double-point needles
   or size needed to obtain gauge
Stitch markers

Gauge
14 sts and 22 rows = 4 inches/10cm in St st with larger
   needles
To save time, take time to check gauge.

Pattern Stitches
1/1 Rib (even number of sts)

Rnd 1: *K1, p1; rep from * around.

Rep Rnd 1 for pat.

Reverse St st (any number of sts)

Purl all rnds.

Lace Panel (panel of 14 sts)

Rnd 1: Yo, k3, ssk, k9.

Rnd 2: K1, yo, k3, ssk, k8.

Rnd 3: K2, yo, k3, ssk, k7.

Rnd 4: K3, yo, k3, ssk, k6.

Rnd 5: K4, yo, k3, ssk, k5.

Rnd 6: K5, yo, k3, ssk, k4.

Rnd 7: K6, yo, k3, ssk, k3.

Rnd 8: K7, yo, k3, ssk, k2.

Rnd 9: K8, yo, k3, ssk, k1.

Rnd 10: K9, yo, k3, ssk.

Rep Rnds 1–10 for Lace Panel.

Beret

With smaller needles, cast on 72 sts. Mark beg of rnd and join without twisting.

Work 5 rnds even in 1/1 Rib pat.

Change to larger needles.

Set-up rnd: [Work 10 sts in Rev St st pat, place marker, work Rnd 1 of Lace Panel pat over next 14 sts, place marker] 3 times.

Note: Slip markers as you come to them.

Work even in established pat until beret measures 5 inches from beg.

Shape top

Notes: Continue established Lace Panel pat in Rnds 1–4 below. Change to dpns when sts no longer fit comfortably on circular needle.

Rnd 1: [P2tog, p6, p2tog, work Lace Panel] 3 times—66 sts.

Rnd 2: [P2tog, p4, p2tog, work Lace Panel] 3 times—60 sts.

Rnd 3: [P2tog, p2, p2tog, work Lace Panel] 3 times—54 sts.

Rnd 4: [P2tog twice, work Lace Panel] 3 times—48 sts.

Rnd 5: [P2, ssk, k10, k2tog] 3 times—42 sts.

Rnd 6: [P2, ssk, k8, k2tog] 3 times—36 sts.

Rnd 7: [P2, ssk, k6, k2tog] 3 times—30 sts.

Rnd 8: [P2, ssk, k4, k2tog] 3 times—24 sts.

Rnd 9: [P2, ssk, k2, k2tog] 3 times—18 sts.

Rnd 10: [P2, ssk, k2tog] 3 times—12 sts.

Rnd 11: [P2tog, remove marker, ssk, remove marker] 3 times—6 sts.

Cut yarn, leaving a 6-inch end. Weave end through rem sts and pull tight to close top of beret.

Block beret over 10-inch dinner plate. ■

Springtime Beret
Sample project was knit with Verde
Collection Sprout (100 per cent organic
cotton) from Classic Elite Yarns.

GARTER DIAMONDS SHAWL

*Are you still a bit leery of lace?
All knit stitches make this
shawl easier than you think.*

Design | Lois Young

Skill Level

INTERMEDIATE

Finished Sizes

22 x 61 inches (22 x 73 inches) Instructions are given for smaller size with larger size in parentheses. When only one number is given, it applies to both sizes.

Materials

Sport weight yarn (327 yds/100g per ball):
  2 (3) balls tan
Size 7 (4.5mm) 29-inch circular and 2 double-point
  (for edging) needles or size needed to obtain gauge
Stitch markers

2
FINE

Gauge

24 sts and 32 rows = 5½ x 4-inch rectangle in pat
  (severely blocked)
To save time, take time to check gauge.

Special Abbreviation

Double yarn over (2yo): Wrap yarn twice around needle; on next row, k1, p1 in each 2yo.

Pattern Stitches

Diamond Eyelet (multiple of 24 sts)

Row 1 (RS): Sl 1, k3, [k2tog, 2yo, ssk] twice, *[k2tog, 2yo, ssk] twice, k8, [k2tog, 2yo, ssk] twice; rep from * to last 12 sts, [k2tog, 2yo, ssk] twice, k3, k1-tbl.

Rows 2, 6, 10, 14, 18, 22, 26 and 30: Sl 1, working (k1, p1) in each 2yo, knit to last st, k1-tbl.

Rows 3, 4, 7, 8, 11, 12, 15, 16, 19, 20, 23, 24, 27, 28 and 31: Sl 1, knit to last st, k1-tbl.

Rows 5 and 29: Sl 1, k5, k2tog, 2yo, ssk, *[k2tog, 2yo, ssk] twice, k4, k2tog, 2yo, ssk, k4, k2tog, 2yo, ssk; rep from * to last 14 sts, [k2tog, 2yo, ssk] twice, k5, k1-tbl.

Rows 9 and 25: Sl 1, k7, *[k2tog, 2yo, ssk] twice, k4; rep from * to last 16 sts, [k2tog, 2yo, ssk] twice, k7, k1-tbl.

Rows 13 and 21: Sl 1, k5, *k4, k2tog, 2yo, ssk, k4, [k2tog, 2yo, ssk] 3 times; rep from * to last 18 sts, k4, k2tog, 2yo, ssk, k9, k1-tbl.

Row 17: Sl 1, k7, *k8, [k2tog, 2yo, ssk] 4 times; rep from * to last 16 sts, k15, k1-tbl.

Row 32: Sl 1, knit to last st, k1-tbl.

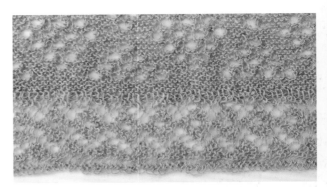

Garter Diamonds Shawl
Sample project was knit with 5 Ply (60 per cent mohair/40 per cent merino wool) from Wagtail Yarns.

Eyelet Edging

Row 1 (RS): K2tog, k1, yo, k3, yo, ssk, k2, yo, p2tog.

Row 2 and all even-numbered rows: Yo, p2tog, knit to last st, sl 1 wyib, pick up and knit 1 st through next st on end of shawl; turn.

Row 3: K2tog (picked-up st and next st), k1, yo, k5, yo, ssk, k1, yo, p2tog.

Row 5: K2tog, k1, yo, k3, yo, ssk, k2, yo, ssk, yo, p2tog.

Row 7: [K2tog] twice, yo, ssk, k3, k2tog, yo, k2, yo, p2tog.

Row 9: [K2tog] twice, yo, ssk, k1, k2tog, yo, k3, yo, p2tog.

Row 11: [K2tog] twice, yo, sl 1, k2tog, psso, yo, k4, yo, p2tog.

Row 12: Yo, p2tog, knit to last st, sl 1 wyib, pick up and knit 1 st through next st on end of shawl; turn.

Rep Rows 1–12 for pat.

Notes

A chart is provided for those preferring to work the Diamond Eyelet pattern stitch from a chart.

For chained edge along the length of the shawl, begin each row with yarn in front, slip first stitch as if to purl, take yarn to back between first and 2nd stitches of row and work across to the last stitch, and then knit last stitch through back loop.

As this shawl is reversible, mark the first row as the right side for ease in remembering which side you are working.

Markers are placed so that they are at the centre of each diamond or diamond-to-be. Keep them in

STITCH KEY
- ☐ K on RS, p on WS
- ⊟ P on RS, k on WS
- ⟋ K2tog
- ⟍ Ssk
- ⊙ Yo
- ⋔ Sl 1
- ୟ K1-tbl

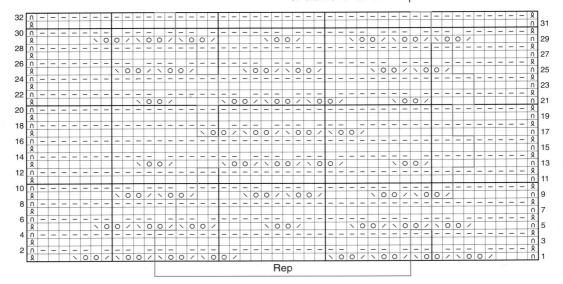

DIAMOND EYELET CHART

this position, including between the double yarn overs when applicable.

Shawl

Body
With circular needle, cast on 96 sts.

Next row: Sl 1, knit across, place marker after every 12 sts, to last st, end k1-tbl.

Knit 4 rows, slipping first st and ending with k1-tbl.

Work [Rows 1–32 of Diamond Eyelet pat] 11 (14) times.

Knit 3 rows, slipping first st and ending with k1-tbl.

Bind off loosely kwise on WS.

Edging
With WS of cast-on edge of shawl facing and 2 dpns, cast on 11 sts, *yo, p2tog, k8, sl 1 wyib, pick up and knit 1 st from shawl edge, turn; k2tog, k10; rep from * once; yo, p2tog, k8, sl 1 wyib, pick up and knit 1 st from shawl edge, turn.

Work Rows 1–12 of Eyelet Edging pat until 3 sts rem along edge of shawl, *yo, p2tog, k8, sl 1 wyib, pick up and knit 1 st from shawl edge, turn; k2tog, k10; rep from * once.

Bind off on WS in kwise.

Rep on bound-off edge of shawl.

Finishing
Weave in all ends on a diagonal. Block severely by pinning out shawl on bedspread or clean carpet. Mist with water from spray bottle, let dry. ∎

CHEVRON LACE GAITER

Gaiters bring warmth and style for both adults and kids.

Design | Eileen Adler

Skill Level

INTERMEDIATE

Finished Size

Approx 21 x 8 inches

Materials

Worsted weight yarn (200 yds per skein):
  1 skein ecru

Size 10 (6mm) straight or 16-inch circular needles
  or size needed to obtain gauge

Stitch markers

Gauge

15 sts and 21 rows = 4 inches/10cm in pat
To save time, take time to check gauge.

Pattern Stitches

Chevron & Eyelet (multiple of 9 sts + 2; worked in rows)

Row 1 (RS): K1, *k4, yo, ssk, k3; rep from * to last st, end k1.

Rows 2, 4 and 6: Purl across.

Row 3: K1, *k2, k2tog, yo, k1, yo, ssk, k2; rep from * to last st, end k1.

Row 5: K1, *k1, k2tog, yo, k3, yo, ssk, k1; rep from * to last st, end k1.

Row 7: K1, *k2tog, yo, k5, yo, ssk; rep from * to last st, end k1.

Row 8: Purl across.

Rep Rows 1–8 for pat.

Chevron & Eyelet (multiple of 9 sts; worked in rnds)

Rnd 1: *K4, yo, ssk, k3; rep from * around.

Rnds 2, 4 and 6: Knit around.

Rnd 3: *K2, k2tog, yo, k1, yo, ssk, k2; rep from * around.

Rnd 5: *K1, k2tog, yo, k3, yo, ssk, k1; rep from * around.

Rnd 7: *K2tog, yo, k5, yo, ssk; rep from * around.

Rnd 8: Knit around.

Rep Rnds 1–8 for pat.

Notes

You will need 7 markers for pattern worked in rows, or 8 markers for pattern worked in rounds; use a different-coloured marker for beginning of round.

Foundation row/round is worked at beginning, but is not counted in 8-row/round pattern repeat.

Gaiter
Worked in rows

Cast on 74 sts.

Foundation row: P1, *p9, place marker; rep from * to last st, end p1.

Work [Rows 1–8 of Chevron & Eyelet pat] 5 times (approx 8 inches).

Bind off all sts.

Assembly

Sew side seam. Block if desired.

Gaiter
Worked in rnds

Cast on 72 sts.

Foundation rnd: *K9, place marker; rep from * around, placing different-coloured marker at end to indicate beg of rnd.

Work [Rnds 1–8 of Chevron and Eyelet pat] 5 times (approx 8 inches).

Bind off all sts.

Block if desired. ■

Chevron Lace Gaiter
Sample project was knit with Lonesome Stone Alpaca (90 per cent alpaca/10 per cent merino) from Lonesome Stone Fiber Mill.

CARIBBEAN SEAS SHAWL

Wrap yourself in waves of softness in this romantic design.

Design | Ava Lynne Green

Skill Level

INTERMEDIATE

Finished Size

Approx 25 x 59 inches (including edging)

Materials

DK weight yarn (131 yds/50g per ball):
  6 balls light blue

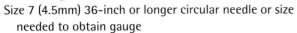

Size 7 (4.5mm) 36-inch or longer circular needle or size needed to obtain gauge

Gauge

14 sts and 25 rows = 4 inches/10cm in pat (blocked)
Exact gauge is not critical to this project.

Notes

Circular needle is used to accommodate large number of stitches. Do not join; work back and forth in rows.

Left edge of right-side rows is the top; cast-on and right edges are short sides.

Shawl

Cast on 132 sts.

Rows 1–6: Knit across.

Row 7 (RS): K3, *yo, k2tog; rep from * to last 3 sts, end k3.

Row 8: K2, k2tog, purl across to last 3 sts, end k3—131 sts.

Row 9: K4, *yo, k2tog; rep from * to last 3 sts, end k3.

Row 10: K2, k2tog, purl across to last 3 sts, end k3—130 sts.

Rep Rows 7–10 until 7 sts rem, ending with a WS row.

Ending corner

Row 1: K7.

Row 2: K2, k2tog, k3—6 sts.

Row 3: K2, k2tog, k2—5 sts.

Row 4: K1, k2tog, k2—4 sts.

Row 5: K1, k2tog, k1—3 sts.

Bind off rem sts.

Ruffle Edging

Note: Edging is worked in rows.

With RS facing, pick up and knit 153 sts along each short side of triangle—306 sts.

Row 1: P3, *yo, p3; rep from * across—306 sts + 102 yo's.

Row 2: K3, *knit into (front, back, front, back) of yo, k3; rep from * across—714 sts.

Row 3: Purl across.

Row 4: Knit across.

Rows 5–12: Continue to work in St st.

Bind off all sts loosely. Block shawl to measurements, allowing trim to form soft ruffles. ■

Caribbean Seas Shawl
Sample project was knit with
Woodland (65 per cent wool/35 per
cent nettles) from Classic Elite Yarns.

JAPANESE LACE VEST

A wavering path leads to wondrous rewards— and a lovely picot trim.

Design | Betsy Dey

Skill Level

INTERMEDIATE

Sizes

Woman's small (medium, large, extra-large, 2X-large) Instructions are given for smallest size, with larger sizes in parentheses. When only one number is given, it applies to all sizes.

Finished Measurements

Chest: 36 (41, 45, 50, 54) inches
Length: 25 (26, 27, 28, 29) inches

Materials

DK weight yarn (136 yds/50g per ball):
  5 (6, 6, 7, 7) balls purple
Size 6 (4mm) 29-inch circular needle or size needed
  to obtain gauge
Stitch holders
Size C/2 (2.75mm) crochet hook
¾-inch button
Spray starch (optional)

3 LIGHT

Gauge

22 sts and 28 rows = 4 inches/10cm in K10, P1 Rib
1 rep of Japanese Lace pat (11 sts) = 2¼ inches
To save time, take time to check gauge.

Pattern Stitches

Japanese Lace (multiple of 11 sts + 7)

Row 1 and all odd-numbered rows: P3, k1, *p10, k1; rep from * to last 3 sts, end p3.

Rows 2, 4, 16 and 18: K3, p1, *k10, p1; rep from * to last 3 sts, end k3.

Rows 6, 10 and 14: K3, p1, *k1, [yo, k1] 3 times, [k2tog-tbl] 3 times, p1; rep from * to last 3 sts, end k3.

Rows 8 and 12: K3, p1, *k1, [k1, yo] 3 times, [k2tog-tbl] 3 times, p1; rep from * to last 3 sts, end k3.

Rows 20 and 24: K3, p1, *[k2tog] 3 times, [k1, yo] 3 times, k1, p1; rep from * to last 3 sts, end k3.

Rows 22 and 26: K3, p1, *[k2tog] 3 times, [yo, k1] 3 times, k1, p1; rep from * to last 3 sts, end k3.

Row 28: K3, p1, *[k2tog] 3 times, [k1, yo] 3 times, k1, p1; rep from * to last 3 sts, end k3.

Rep Rows 1–28 for pat.

Picot Edging

Row 1 (WS): Knit across.

Row 2: Bind off 2 sts, *slip rem st back to LH needle, cast on 2 sts, bind off 5 sts; rep from * across.

Notes

Vest is knit in 1 piece from bottom to underarms in Japanese Lace pat, and then divided for front and back yokes and worked by repeating Rows 1 and 2. The stitch pattern forms a wavy front.

Circular needle is used to accommodate large number of stitches. Do not join; work back and forth in rows.

Vest

Body

Cast on 183 (205, 227, 249, 271) sts. [Rep Rows 1–28 of Japanese Lace pat] 3 times, and then work Rows 1–3 once more.

Divide for fronts & back

Slip first and last 47 (53, 58, 64, 69) sts to holders.

Back

With RS facing, attach yarn to back. Maintaining established pat, work Japanese Lace pat Rows 1 and 2 across rem 89 (99, 111, 121, 133) sts.

Japanese Lace Vest
Sample project was knit with Grace (100 per cent mercerized cotton) from Patons Yarn.

Shape armholes

Note: Work yokes by rep Japanese Lace pat Rows 1 and 2 throughout.

Bind off at beg of row [6 sts] twice, then [3 sts] twice—71 (81, 93, 103, 115) sts.

Work in pat until back measures 9 (10, 11, 12, 13) inches from underarms. Place first 23 (25, 29, 33, 37) sts on holder for shoulder, bind off centre 25 (31, 35, 37, 41) sts and place rem 23 (25, 29, 33, 37) sts on 2nd holder for 2nd shoulder.

Fronts

With RS facing, attach separate balls of yarn to fronts. Working both sides at once and maintaining pat, work pat Rows 1 and 2 across fronts.

Shape armholes & neck

Bind off at each armhole [6 sts] once, then [3 sts] once, and *at the same time*, at neck edge [k3tog] once, then dec 1 st [every RS row] 4 times, then [every other RS row] 9 (13, 14, 16, 17) times—23 (25, 29, 33, 37) sts rem.

Work even if needed until fronts measure same as back to shoulder. Place rem shoulder sts on holders.

Assembly

Bind off front and back shoulders, using 3-needle bind-off (see page 27).

Roll front St st edges to inside and whipstitch in place, being careful not to pull too tight.

Bottom Edging

With RS facing, pick up and knit 1 st in each st across lower edge. Work Picot Edging.

Neck Edging

Beg at right front neck shaping with RS facing, pick up and knit 2 sts for every 3 rows to shoulder, 1 st for every st across back neck and 2 sts for every 3 rows to beg of left front neck shaping. Work Picot Edging.

Armhole Edging

Beg at underarm with RS facing, pick up and knit 1 st for each st and 2 sts for every 3 rows around armhole. Work Picot Edging.

Button Loop

With crochet hook, join yarn at k3tog on right front, ch 10, join and fasten off. Sew button opposite loop.

Block, taking particular care to shape wavy front edges. Starch edges, if desired. ■

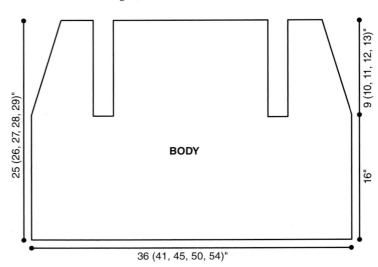

BODY

25 (26, 27, 28, 29)"

9 (10, 11, 12, 13)"

16"

36 (41, 45, 50, 54)"

LACE SHOPPING BAG

Hold the plastic and save a tree: take this handy and beautiful bag to the market instead.

Design | Cecily Glowik MacDonald

Skill Level

INTERMEDIATE

Finished Size

Approx 15 x 28½ inches (excluding handle)

Materials

DK weight yarn (110 yds/50g per ball):
  5 balls green
Size 5 (3.75mm) 24-inch circular needle
Size 7 (4.5mm) 16- and 24-inch circular and set of
  double-point needles or size needed to obtain gauge
Stitch markers

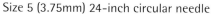

Gauge

18 sts and 24 rows = 4 inches/10cm in Lace pat with
  larger needles
To save time, take time to check gauge.

Pattern Stitches

K1, P1 Rib (multiple of 2 sts; worked in rnds)

Rnd 1: *K1, p1; rep from * around.

Rep Rnd 1 for pat.

K1, P1 Rib (multiple of 2 sts; worked in rows)

Row 1: Sl 1 pwise, k1, *p1, k1; rep from * across.

Rep Row 1 for pat.

Lace (multiple of 9 sts)

Rnd 1: *K2tog, [k1, yo] twice, k1, ssk, p2; rep from * around.

Rnd 2 and all even-numbered rnds: *K7, p2; rep from * around.

Rnd 3: *K2tog, yo, k3, yo, ssk, p2; rep from * around.

Rnd 5: *K1, yo, ssk, k1, k2tog, yo, k1, p2; rep from * around.

Rnd 7: *K2, yo, sl 1, k2tog, psso, yo, k2, p2; rep from * around.

Rnd 8: Rep Rnd 2.

Rep Rnds 1–8 for Lace pat.

Notes

Bag is worked from top opening to bottom; handle is added after bag body is finished.

When shaping bottom of bag, use markers in a different colour than the beginning of round marker. Change to 16-inch circular needles, and then double-point needles as needed.

Bag

Body

With smaller 24-inch circular needle, cast on 126 sts, join without twisting and place marker for beg of rnd. Work in K1, P1 Rib in rnds until piece measures 1½ inches.

Change to larger 24-inch circular needle and beg pat, work 8 reps of Lace pat, ending with Rnd 7 of last rep.

Next rnd (Rnd 8): *Slip marker, work 14 sts in pat, place different-coloured marker; rep from * around.

Dec rnd: *Slip marker, knit to 2 sts before next marker, k2tog; rep from * around.

Next rnd: Purl around.

Rep last 2 rnds until 1 st rem between markers. Purl 1 rnd, removing all markers except beg of rnd marker.

Next rnd: *K2tog; rep from * to last st, end k1—5 sts rem.

With tapestry needle, thread yarn through rem sts and pull tight to close bottom of bag.

Handle

With larger needles, cast on 8 sts and work K1, P1 Rib in rows until piece measures approx 25 inches or desired length. Bind off all sts in pat.

Sew cast-on edge of handle to bottom of ribbing inside bag, sew sides for extra strength; sew bound-off end of handle inside opposite side of bag. Block if desired. ■

Lace Shopping Bag
Sample project was knit with Pebbles (75 per cent cotton/25 per cent acrylic) from Classic Elite Yarns.

BREAD-BASKET LACE COVER

Nothing says "Welcome to your new home!" like homemade bread and a lovely lace cover.

Design | Nazanin S. Fard

Skill Level

INTERMEDIATE

Finished Size
Approx 16 inches square

Materials
Size 10 crochet cotton (400 yds per ball): 1 ball white
Size 1 (2.25mm) straight and 40-inch circular knitting needles
Size 7 (1.65mm) steel crochet hook
Stitch marker
Rustproof pins
Blocking board

Gauge
Gauge is not critical to this project.

Special Abbreviation
Slip, knit 2 together, pass (sk2p): Slip next st, k2tog, pass slipped st over k2tog and off needle to dec 2 sts.

Notes
Slip the first stitch of each row purlwise to make it easier to pick up stitches when working on the edging.

Charts for centre pattern and edging are included for those preferring to work pattern stitches from a chart. Only right-side rows are included on centre chart. Wrong-side rows are worked as: Slip 1 purlwise, purl across.

Cover

Centre
Cast on 87 sts.

Row 1 and all odd-numbered rows (WS): Sl 1pwise, purl across.

Row 2: Sl 1pwise, *k1, yo, ssk, k3, yo, ssk, k2, k2tog, yo; rep from * across to last 2 sts, k2.

Row 4: Sl 1pwise, *k1, yo, ssk, k1, k2tog, yo, k1, yo, ssk, k1, k2tog, yo; rep from * across to last 2 sts, k2.

Row 6: Sl 1pwise, *k1, yo, ssk, k2tog, yo, k3, yo, ssk, k2tog, yo; rep from * to last 2 sts, k2.

Row 8: Sl 1pwise, *k1, yo, ssk, k7, k2tog, yo; rep from * across to last 2 sts, k2.

Rep [Rows 1–8] 13 times. Do not bind off.

Edging
Rnd 1: Knit across, inc 1 st in last st, place marker, pick up and knit 88 sts on each rem side placing markers at each corner—352 sts.

Rnd 2: *Yo, [k1, yo, ssk, k5, k2tog, yo] to 2 sts before marker, k1, yo, k1; rep from * around—360 sts.

Rnd 3 and all odd-numbered rnds: Purl around.

Rnd 4: *Yo, k1, [k2, yo, ssk, k3, k2tog, yo, k1] to 3 sts before marker, k2, yo, k1; rep from * around—368 sts.

Rnd 6: *Yo, k2, [k3, yo, ssk, k1, k2tog, yo, k2] to 4 sts before marker, k3, yo, k1; rep from * around—376 sts.

Rnd 8: *Yo, k3, [k4, yo, sk2p, yo, k3] to 5 sts before marker, k4, yo, k1; rep from * around—384 sts.

Rnd 10: *Insert crochet hook into each of next 4 sts and remove sts from knitting needle, yo and pull through all loops on hook (sc dec made), ch 9 (see page 25); rep from * around, join in first sc dec. Fasten off.

Finishing

Spread out piece on blocking board and pin tight to size. Let dry. ∎

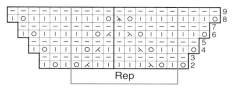

CENTRE LACE CHART

Note: *WS rows not shown on chart are worked as follows: Sl 1pwise, purl across.*

EDGING LACE CHART

STITCH KEY
- I K on RS, p on WS
- − P on RS, k on WS
- O Yo
- ⟋ K2tog
- ⟍ Ssk
- • Sl 1pwise
- ⋏ Sk2p

Bread-Basket Lace Cover
Sample project was knit with Traditions (100 per cent mercerized cotton) from DMC.

ROSEBUDS THROW

Pamper yourself with this soft, lacy throw or make it for someone special.

Design | Frances Hughes

Skill Level

INTERMEDIATE

Finished Size

44 x 52 inches (excluding fringe)

Materials

Worsted weight yarn (153 yds/50g per ball):
  6 balls pink

Size 10.5 (6.5mm) 29-inch circular needle or size needed to obtain gauge

4 MEDIUM

Gauge

13 sts = 4 inches/10cm in pat

To save time, take time to check gauge.

Note

Circular needle is used to accommodate large number of stitches. Work back and forth in rows, do not join.

Throw

Cast on 143 sts.

Knit 2 rows for border.

Row 1: K3, *yo, p1, p3tog, p1, yo, k1; rep from * to last 2 sts, k2.

Rows 2, 4 and 6: K2, purl to last 2 sts, k2.

Row 3: K4, yo, sl 1, k2tog, psso, yo, *k3, yo, sl 1, k2tog, psso, yo; rep from * to last 4 sts, k4.

Row 5: K2, p2tog, p1, yo, k1, yo, p1, *p3tog, p1, yo, k1, yo, p1; rep from * to last 4 sts, p2tog, k2.

Row 7: K2, k2tog, yo, k3, yo, *sl 1, k2tog, psso, yo, k3, yo; rep from * to last 4 sts, sl 1, k1, psso, k2.

Row 8: K2, purl to last 2 sts, k2.

Rep Rows 1–8 until piece measures approx 52 inches, ending with Row 8.

Knit 2 rows for upper border.

Bind off all sts.

Fringe

Referring to single-knot fringe instructions on page 50, cut 8 (12-inch) lengths of yarn for each fringe. Work across cast-on and bound-off ends, placing knots at each corner, and spacing rem knots in every 10th st across, for a total of 15 at each end.

Block lightly. ■

Rosebuds Throw
Sample project was knit with
Ingenua by Fil Katia (78 per cent
mohair/13 per cent nylon/9 per
cent wool) from Knitting Fever.

LACE STAR CANDLE MAT

Create a family heirloom worthy of Grandma.

Design | Nazanin S. Fard

Skill Level
INTERMEDIATE

Finished Size
Approx 14 inches across (after blocking)

Materials
Size 10 crochet cotton (400 yds per ball): 2 balls ecru
Size 1 (2.25mm) set of 5 double-point needles and 16-inch circular needle or size needed to obtain gauge
Size 7 (1.65mm) steel crochet hook
Stitch marker
Rustproof pins
Spray starch or fabric stiffener
Blocking board

Gauge
15 sts = 2 inches/5cm in pat
To save time, take time to check gauge.

Special Abbreviation
Slip, knit 2 together, pass (sk2p): Slip next st, k2tog, pass slipped st over k2tog and off needle to dec 2 sts.

Notes
Candle mat is worked in rounds starting at the centre with double-point needles and changing to a circular needle as necessary to accommodate increased number of stitches.

Place a marker at the beginning of the round. Slip marker when you come to it on following rounds.

Candle Mat
Cast 3 sts onto each of 4 needles; use 5th needle for working—12 sts.

Rnd 1: Knit around.

Rnd 2: *Yo, k1; rep from * around—24 sts.

Rnds 3 and 4: Knit around.

Rnd 5: *Yo, k1; rep from * around—48 sts.

Rnds 6–8: Knit around.

Rnd 9: *Yo, k1; rep from * around—96 sts.

Rnds 10–14: Knit around.

Rnd 15: *Yo, k12; rep from * around—104 sts.

Rnd 16 and all rem even-numbered rnds: Knit around.

Rnd 17: *K1, yo, ssk, k8, k2tog, yo; rep from * around.

Rnd 19: *[K1, yo] twice, ssk, k6, k2tog, yo, k1, yo; rep from * around—120 sts.

Rnd 21: *[K1, yo] 4 times, ssk, k4, k2tog, yo, [k1, yo] 3 times; rep from * around—168 sts.

Rnd 23: *K4, [yo, ssk] 3 times, k2, [k2tog, yo] 3 times, k3; rep from * around.

Rnd 25: *K1, yo, k4, [yo, ssk] 3 times, [k2tog, yo] 3 times, k4, yo; rep from * around—184 sts.

Lace Star Candle Mat
Sample project was knit
with Traditions (100 per cent
mercerized cotton) from DMC.

Rnd 27: *[K1, yo] twice, k3, [ssk, yo] 3 times, [k2tog, yo] 3 times, k2tog, k3, yo, k1, yo; rep from * around—208 sts.

Rnd 29: *K1, yo, ssk, yo, k1, yo, k5, [yo, ssk] twice, yo, k1, yo, [k2tog, yo] twice, k5, yo, k1, yo, k2tog, yo; rep from * around—256 sts.

Rnd 31: *K2, [yo, ssk] twice, yo, k6, [yo, ssk] twice, k1, [k2tog, yo] twice, k6, yo, [k2tog, yo] twice, k1; rep from * around—272 sts.

Rnd 33: *K1, [yo, ssk] 4 times, k5, yo, ssk, yo, sk2p, yo, k2tog, yo, k5, [k2tog, yo] 4 times; rep from * around.

Rnd 35: *K2, [yo, ssk] 4 times, k5, yo, ssk, k1, k2tog, yo, k5, [k2tog, yo] 4 times, k1; rep from * around.

Rnd 37: *K1, [yo, ssk] 5 times, k5, yo, sk2p, yo, k5, [k2tog, yo] 5 times; rep from * around.

Rnd 39: *K2, [yo, ssk] 5 times, k4, sk2p, k4, [k2tog, yo] 5 times, k1; rep from * around—256 sts.

Rnd 41: *K1, [yo, ssk] 6 times, k7, [k2tog, yo] 6 times; rep from * around.

Rnd 43: *K2, [yo, ssk] 6 times, k5, [k2tog, yo] 6 times, k1; rep from * around.

Rnd 45: *K1, [yo, ssk] 7 times, k3, [k2tog, yo] 7 times; rep from * around.

Rnd 47: *K2, [yo, ssk] 7 times, k1, [k2tog, yo] 7 times, k1; rep from * around.

Rnd 49: *K1, [yo, ssk] 7 times, yo, sk2p, yo, [k2tog, yo] 7 times; rep from * around.

Rnds 50–52: Knit around.

Rnd 53: *Insert crochet hook into each of next 4 sts and remove sts from knitting needle, yo and pull through all loops on hook (sc dec made), ch 9 (see page 25); rep from * around, join in first sc dec. Fasten off.

Finishing
Spray lightly with starch or fabric stiffener.

Spread on blocking board, stretch to shape and pin the chain loops in place until dry. ■

LACE LEAF SOCKS

Keep your toes warm and comfy in these hand-knit socks. You'll want to make several pairs in your favourite colours.

Design | E.J. Slayton

Skill Level

INTERMEDIATE

Sizes

Women's small/medium (large) Instructions are given for smaller size, with larger size in parentheses. When only one number is given, it applies to both sizes.

Finished Measurements

Top length: 7½ (8) inches
Foot length: 9¼ (10) inches

Materials

DK weight yarn (132 yds/50g per ball):
  2 (3) balls red
Size 3 (3.25mm) double-point needles or size needed
  to obtain gauge
Heel and toe reinforcement (optional)
Stitch markers
Safety pin

Gauge

13 sts and 16 rnds = 2 inches/5cm in St st
To save time, take time to check gauge.

Special Abbreviation

Make 1 (M1): Inc by making a backward loop over the right needle.

Sock

Cast on 48 (52) sts. Join, being careful not to twist, and work in k2, p2 rib for 2 inches and on last rnd, inc 1 (2) st(s) (evenly around)—49 (54) sts.

Set-up rnd: K0 (2), p1 (2), [k3, p2] 4 times, place marker, k7, place marker, [p2, k3] 4 times, p1 (2), k0 (1). Slip first st to Needle 3 (slip last st to Needle 1) so that next rnd begins with k3.

Rnd 1: *Pass 3rd st over first 2 sts, k1, yo, k1, p2*; rep from * to marker, k2tog, k1, [yo, k1] twice, ssk, p2; rep between * to end of rnd.

Rnds 2, 4, 6 and 8: *K3, p2*; rep from * to marker, k7, p2; rep between * to end of rnd.

Rnd 3: *K3, p2*; rep from * to marker, k2tog, yo, k3, yo, ssk, p2; rep between * to end of rnd.

Rnd 5: *Pass 3rd st over first 2 sts, k1, yo, k1, p2*; rep from * to marker, k1, yo, ssk, k1, k2tog, yo, k1, p2, rep between * to end of rnd.

Rnd 7: *K3, p2*; rep from * to marker, k2, yo, sl 2 kwise, k1, p2sso, yo, k2, p2; rep between * to end of rnd.

Rep Rnds 1–8 for pat until top measures 7½ (8) inches or desired length.

Heel

Knit across next 11 (15) sts; divide next 25 (27) sts centred on leaf pat on 2 needles for instep; slip rem 13 (12) sts to beg of first needle. Turn and purl across, inc 1 (0) in centre—25 (27) heel sts.

Row 1 (RS): Sl 1, *k1, sl 1, rep from * across.

Row 2: Purl.

Rows 3–23 (25): Rep Rows 1 and 2, ending with Row 1.

Shape heel

Place safety pin marker in st 13 (14). Shaping takes place evenly spaced on each side of this centre st.

Row 1 (WS): P15 (16), p2tog, p1, turn.

Row 2: Sl 1, k6, k2tog, k1, turn.

Row 3: Sl 1, p7, p2tog, p1, turn.

Row 4: Sl 1, k8, k2tog, k1, turn.

Continue to work in this manner, having 1 more st before dec each row until all sts have been worked, ending with a RS row—15 (17) sts rem.

Instep

Using needle containing rem heel sts, pick up and knit 12 (13) sts in loops along edge of heel flap (Needle 1); with free needle, k2 (3), place marker, work in pat across 21 sts, place marker, k2 (3) [25 (27) instep sts on Needle 2]; pick up and knit 12 (13) sts in loops along edge of heel flap, with same needle, k7 (8) sts from Needle 1 [19 (21) sts on Needle 3]—64 (70) sts.

Rnd 1: Knit to marker, work 21 sts in established pat, knit to end.

Rnd 2: Knit to last 3 sts on Needle 1, k2tog, k1; work across Needle 2 in established pat; at beg of Needle 3, k1, ssk, knit to end.

Rep Rnds 1 and 2 until a total of 25 (27) sts rem on Needles 1 and 3, then work even in established pat until foot measures 7¼ (8) inches or approximately 2 inches less than desired length.

Toe

Rnd 1: Knit.

Rnd 2: Knit to last 3 sts on Needle 1, k2tog, k1; on Needle 2, k1, ssk, knit to last 3 sts, k2tog, k1; on Needle 3, k1, ssk, knit to end.

Rep Rnds 1 and 2 until 22 sts rem. With Needle 3, knit across sts from Needle 1—11 sts each on 2 needles.

Weave toe

Cut yarn, leaving an 18-inch end. Join sts using Kitchener st (see page 24). ■

Lace Leaf Socks
Sample project was knit with Sedrun
(90 per cent wool/10 per cent nylon)
from Forelich Wolle.

LACY LEAVES TUNIC

This soft lace tunic will fit into your summer wardrobe with smooth style.

Design | Svetlana Avrakh

Skill Level

INTERMEDIATE

Sizes

Woman's small (medium, large, extra-large, 2X-large) Instructions are given for smallest size, with larger sizes in parentheses. When only one number is given, it applies to all sizes.

Finished Measurements

Chest: 36 (40, 44, 48, 52) inches
Length: 23 (23½, 24, 25, 25) inches

Materials

Sport weight yarn (237 yds/85g per ball):
  4 (5, 5, 6, 7) balls ecru
Size 5 (3.75mm) needles
Size 6 (4mm) needles or size needed to obtain gauge
Stitch holders
Stitch markers

Gauge

22 sts and 28 rows = 4 inches/10cm in St st with larger
  needles
To save time, take time to check gauge.

Tunic

Back/Front

Make 2

With larger needles, cast on 97 (109, 121, 133, 145) sts.

Row 1 (RS): [Ssk, yo] 0 (3, 2, 1, 4) time(s), p1, *[ssk, yo] 3 times, k1, p1, yo, k2, ssk, k3, p1; rep from * to last 0 (6, 4, 2, 8) sts, end [ssk, yo] 0 (2, 1, 0, 3) time(s), k0 (2, 2, 2, 2).

Row 2 and all even-numbered rows: P0 (6, 4, 2, 8), *k1, p7; rep from * to last 1 (7, 5, 3, 9) st(s), end k1, p0 (6, 4, 2, 8).

Row 3: [Ssk, yo] 0 (3, 2, 1, 4) time(s), p1, *[ssk, yo] 3 times, k1, p1, k1, yo, k2, ssk, k2, p1; rep from * to last 0 (6, 4, 2, 8) sts, end [ssk, yo] 0 (2, 1, 0, 3) time(s), k0 (2, 2, 2, 2).

Row 5: [Ssk, yo] 0 (3, 2, 1, 4) time(s), p1, *[ssk, yo] 3 times, k1, p1, k2, yo, k2, ssk, k1, p1; rep from * to last 0 (6, 4, 2, 8) sts, end [ssk, yo] 0 (2, 1, 0, 3) time(s), k0 (2, 2, 2, 2).

Row 7: [Ssk, yo] 0 (3, 2, 1, 4) time(s), p1, *[ssk, yo] 3 times, k1, p1, k3, yo, k2, ssk, p1; rep from * to last 0 (6, 4, 2, 8) sts, end [ssk, yo] 0 (2, 1, 0, 3) time(s), k0 (2, 2, 2, 2).

Row 8: Rep Row 2.

Rows 9–16: Rep Rows 1–8.

Row 17: K0 (1, 1, 1, 1), [yo, k2tog] 0 (2, 1, 0, 3) time(s), k0 (1, 1, 1, 1), p1, *k3, k2tog, k2, yo, p1, k1, [yo, k2tog] 3 times, p1; rep from * to last 0 (6, 4, 2, 8) sts, end [yo, k2tog] 0 (3, 2, 1, 4) time(s).

Row 19: K0 (1, 1, 1, 1), [yo, k2tog] 0 (2, 1, 0, 3) time(s), k0 (1, 1, 1, 1), p1, *k2, k2tog, k2, yo, k1, p1, k1, [yo, k2tog] 3 times, p1; rep from * to last 0 (6, 4, 2, 8) sts, end [yo, k2tog] 0 (3, 2, 1, 4) time(s).

Lacy Leaves Tunic
Sample project was knit with Satin Sport (100 per cent acrylic) from Bernat.

Row 21: K0 (1, 1, 1, 1), [yo, k2tog] 0 (2, 1, 0, 3) time(s), k0 (1, 1, 1, 1), p1, *k1, k2tog, k2, yo, k2, p1, k1, [yo, k2tog] 3 times, p1; rep from * to last 0 (6, 4, 2, 8) sts, end [yo, k2tog] 0 (3, 2, 1, 4) time(s).

Row 23: K0 (1, 1, 1, 1), [yo, k2tog] 0 (2, 1, 0, 3) time(s), k0 (1, 1, 1, 1), p1, *k2tog, k2, yo, k3, p1, k1, [yo, k2tog] 3 times, p1; rep from * to last 0 (6, 4, 2, 8) sts, end [yo, k2tog] 0 (3, 2, 1, 4) time(s).

Row 24: Rep Row 2.

Rows 25–32: Rep Rows 17–24.

Rep Rows 1–32 of pat until piece measures 15 inches from beg, ending with a RS row.

Shape cap sleeves

Inc 1 st at each edge on next row, then [every other row] 2 (4, 4, 4, 5) times more, then [every row] 3 times, working inc sts into [ssk, yo] or [yo, k2tog] pat—109 (125, 137, 149, 163) sts. Place markers at each end of last row.

Continue to work even in pat as set until piece measures 4 (4½, 5, 6, 6) inches from marked row, ending with a WS row.

Left Yoke

Row 1 (RS): Work in pat across 46 (53, 59, 64, 69) sts, turn. Leave rem sts on a spare needle.

Row 2: Bind off 4 sts, work in pat to end of row.

Rows 3, 5 and 7: Work in pat to last 2 sts, k2tog.

Row 4: Bind off 3 sts, work in pat to end of row.

Row 6: Bind off 2 sts, work in pat to end of row.

Row 8: P2tog, work in pat to end of row.

Row 9: Work in pat to last 2 sts, work 2 sts tog—32 (39, 45, 50, 55) sts.

Work 5 rows even in pat.

Shape shoulder

Bind off 4 (5, 6, 7, 8) sts at beg of next row, then [every other row] 4 times. Work 1 row even. Bind off rem 12 (14, 15, 15, 15) sts.

Right Yoke

With RS facing, slip next 17 (19, 19, 21, 25) sts to a holder for neck.

Row 1: Join yarn to rem sts and work in pat to end of row.

Rows 2, 4, 6 and 8: Work in pat to last 2 sts, end p2tog.

Row 3: Bind off 4 sts, work in pat to end of row.

Row 5: Bind off 3 sts, work in pat to end of row.

Row 7: Bind off 2 sts, work in pat to end of row.

Row 9: Ssk, work in pat to end of row—32 (39, 45, 50, 55) sts.

Work 6 rows even in pat.

Shape shoulder

Bind off 4 (5, 6, 7, 8) sts at beg of next row, then [every other row] 4 times more. Work 1 row even. Bind off rem 12 (14, 15, 15, 15) sts.

Assembly

Pin garment pieces to measurements. Cover with a damp cloth, leaving cloth to dry.

Neckband

Sew right shoulder seam. With RS facing and smaller needles, pick up and knit 22 sts along left front neck edge, k17 (19, 19, 21, 25) from holder; pick up and knit 22 sts along right front neck edge, 22 sts along right back neck edge, k17 (19, 19, 21, 25) from holder; pick up and knit 22 sts along left back neck edge—122 (126, 126, 130, 138) sts.

Picot Bind-Off: Bind off 2 sts, *place rem st on LH needle, cable cast-on (see page 27) 3 sts, pass 2nd, 3rd and 4th sts over first st, place rem st on RH needle, bind off 3 sts; rep from * across. Fasten off.

Armhole Edging

Sew left shoulder seam. With RS facing and smaller needles, pick up and knit 70 (76, 80, 94, 94) sts. Work Picot Bind-Off as for neckband.

Bottom Edging

Sew left side seam from bottom to armhole marker. With RS facing and smaller needles, pick up and knit 188 (216, 240, 264, 288) sts along cast-on edge. Work Picot Bind-Off as for neckband.

Sew right side seam from bottom to armhole marker.

Twisted Cord

Cut 4 (92-inch-long) strands of yarn. Knot strands tog at 1 end, tie end to door handle or hook. Twist strands in 1 direction until yarn kinks up on itself when relaxed. Hold yarn at middle of twisted strand, remove end from door handle and allow yarn to twist onto itself. Tie a knot at each end and trim, leaving approx 1 inch for tassel. Beg and ending at centre front, thread twisted cord through eyelet holes of pat along waist. ∎

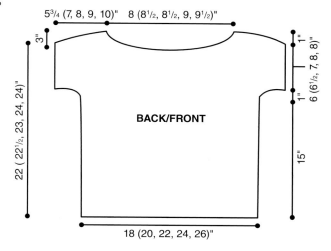

5³⁄₄ (7, 8, 9, 10)"   8 (8¹⁄₂, 8¹⁄₂, 9, 9¹⁄₂)"

3"

1" 1"

6 (6¹⁄₂, 7, 8, 8)"

22 (22¹⁄₂, 23, 24, 24)"

1"

BACK/FRONT

15"

18 (20, 22, 24, 26)"

SPRING FLOWERS CARDIGAN

Delicate little flowers bloom on this short-sleeved V-neck cardigan.

Design | E.J. Slayton

Skill Level

INTERMEDIATE

Sizes

Woman's small (medium, large, extra-large, 2X-large) Instructions are given for smallest size, with larger sizes in parentheses. When only one number is given, it applies to all sizes.

Finished Measurements

Chest: 38 (42, 46, 50, 54) inches
Length: 23 (23½, 24, 24½, 25) inches

Materials

Worsted weight yarn (120 yds/50g per ball):
  7 (8, 9, 10, 11) balls coral
Size 4 (3.5mm) 24- or 29-inch circular needle
Size 6 (4mm) needles or size needed to obtain gauge
Stitch markers
Stitch holders
5 (¼-inch) buttons

Gauge

20 sts and 26 rows = 4 inches/10cm in pat with larger needles
To save time, take time to check gauge.

Special Abbreviation

Make 1 (M1): Inc by making a backward loop over RH needle.

Pattern Stitches

K1, P1 Rib (odd number of sts)

Row 1 (WS): K1, *p1, k1; rep from * across.

Row 2: K2, *p1, k1; rep from * to last st, end k1.

Rep Rows 1 and 2 for rib.

Spring Flowers (multiple of 14 sts)

Row 1 (RS): *K1, yo, k1, ssk, k7, k2tog, k1, yo; rep from * across.

Row 2: Purl across.

Row 3: *P1, k1, yo, k1, ssk, k5, k2tog, k1, yo, k1; rep from * across.

Rows 4 and 6: *P13, k1; rep from * across.

Row 5: *P1, k13; rep from * across.

Row 7: *Yo, k2tog, k12; rep from * across.

Row 8: Purl across.

Row 9: *K4, k2tog, k1, [yo, k1] twice, ssk, k3; rep from * across.

Row 10: Purl across.

Row 11: *K3, k2tog, k1, yo, k1, p1, k1, yo, k1, ssk, k2; rep from * across.

Rows 12 and 14: *P6, k1, p7; rep from * across.

Spring Flowers Cardigan
Sample project was knit with
Bristol Yarn Gallery Somerset (85
per cent pima cotton/15 per cent
silk) from Plymouth Yarn Co.

Row 13: *K7, p1, k6; rep from * across.

Row 15: *K7, yo, k2tog, k5; rep from * across.

Row 16: Purl across.

Rep Rows 1–16 for pat.

Notes
Instructions include edge stitches on each side as noted which are not shown on chart. Work edge stitches in stockinette stitch.

Work all increases and decreases 1 stitch in from edge.

When working Spring Flowers pattern, work in stockinette stitch when there aren't enough stitches for a yarn over and its accompanying decrease.

Cardigan

Back
With smaller needles, cast on 89 (99, 107, 117, 127) sts and work 10 rows in K1, P1 Rib.

Inc row (WS): Purl, inc 8 (8, 10, 10, 10) sts evenly across—97 (107, 117, 127, 137) sts.

Change to larger needles.

Beg pat: K2 (4, 2, 3, 5), place marker, beg and end as indicated on Back/Front chart, work Row 1 of pat to last 2 (4, 2, 3, 5) sts, place marker, k2 (4, 2, 3, 5).

Keeping edge sts in St st, work pat between markers until back measures 14 inches from beg, ending with a WS row.

Shape armholes
Bind off 5 (8, 9, 13, 16) sts at beg of next 2 rows, then dec 1 st at each side [every RS row] 5 (5, 6, 6, 6) times—77 (81, 87, 89, 93) sts.

Work even in pat until armhole measures 8 (8½, 9, 9½, 10) inches, ending with a WS row.

Shape shoulders
Bind off at beg of row [7 (8, 7, 7, 8) sts] twice, then [7 (7, 8, 8, 8) sts] 4 times. Place rem 35 (37, 41, 43, 45) sts on holder for back neck.

Left Front
With smaller needles, cast on 45 (51, 55, 61, 65) sts and work 10 rows in K1, P1 Rib.

Inc row (WS): Purl, inc 5 (4, 5, 4, 5) sts evenly across—50 (55, 60, 65, 70) sts.

Beg pat: Change to larger needles, k2 (4, 2, 3, 5), place marker, beg and end as indicated on Back/Front chart, work Row 1 of pat to last st, place marker, k1.

Note: On Row 7 of pat, omit yo, k2tog at front edge.

Keeping edge sts in St st, work in pat until front measures 12½ inches from beg.

Shape neck & armhole
Beg on next RS row, at end of RS rows, dec 1 st by k2tog [every other row] 12 (14, 18, 19, 20) times, then [every 4th row] 7 (6, 4, 4, 4) times, and *at the same time*, when front measures 14 inches, bind off 5 (8, 9, 13, 16) sts at beg of next WS row, then dec 1 st at armhole edge [every RS row] 5 (5, 6, 6, 6) times—21 (22, 23, 23, 24) sts rem when all dec are completed.

Work even until front measures same as back to shoulder, ending with a WS row.

Shape shoulder

Bind off at beg of RS rows (armhole edge) [7 (8, 7, 7, 8) sts] once, then [7 (7, 8, 8, 8) sts] twice.

Right Front

With smaller needles, cast on 45 (51, 55, 51, 65) sts and work 10 rows in K1, P1 Rib.

Inc row (WS): Purl, inc 5 (4, 5, 4, 5) sts evenly across 50 (55, 60, 65, 70) sts.

Beg pat: Change to larger needles, k1, beg and end as indicated on Back/Front chart, work Row 1 of pat to last 2 (3, 1, 3, 4) st(s), place marker, k2 (3, 1, 3, 4).

Note: On Row 7 of pat, omit yo, k2tog at front edge.

Keeping edge sts in St st, work in pat until front measures 12½ inches from beg.

Shape neck & armhole

Beg on next RS row, at beg of RS rows, dec 1 st by ssk [every other row] 12 (14, 18, 19, 20) times, then [every 4th row] 7 (6, 4, 4, 4) times, and *at the same time,* when front measures 14 inches, at beg of next RS row, bind off 5 (8, 9, 13, 16) sts, then dec 1 st at armhole edge [every RS row] 5 (5, 6, 6, 6) times—21 (22, 23, 23, 24) sts rem when all dec are completed.

Work even until front measures same as back to shoulder, ending with a RS row.

Shape shoulder

Bind off at beg of WS rows (armhole edge) [7 (8, 7, 7, 8) sts] once, then [7 (7, 8, 8, 8)] sts twice.

Sleeves

With smaller needles, cast on 65 (69, 73, 77, 83) sts and work 10 rows in K1, P1 Rib.

Inc row (WS): Purl, inc 4 (4, 6, 6, 6) sts evenly across— 69 (73, 79, 83, 89) sts.

Change to larger needles.

Beg pat: K2, place marker, beg and end as indicated on Sleeve chart, work Row 1 of pat to last 2 sts, place marker, k2.

Keeping edge sts in St st, work pat between markers, and *at the same time,* inc 1 st at each edge [every 4th row] 6 times, working added sts into pat—81 (85, 91, 95, 101) sts.

Work even until sleeve measures 5 inches from beg, ending with a WS row.

Shape cap

Bind off 5 (8, 9, 13, 16) sts at beg of next 2 rows, work 4 (0, 2, 4, 8) rows even, dec 1 st at each side [every RS row] 12 (11, 13, 13, 12) times, [every row] 5 (5, 3, 1, 1) time(s), then bind off 4 sts at beg of next 6 rows. Bind off rem 13 (13, 17, 17, 19) sts.

Assembly

Sew shoulder seams. Mark right front for 5 buttonholes, with first approx ½ inch above bottom, last at beg of neck shaping, and rem 3 evenly spaced between.

Front Band

Beg at right front corner with smaller circular needle, RS facing, pick up and knit 2 sts for every 3 rows along front to shoulder, placing a marker at beg of neck shaping, knit across back neck sts, dec 4 sts evenly across, pick up and knit along left front to match right front.

Rows 1 and 3 (WS): Sl 1, knit across.

Row 2: Sl 1, knit to marker, slip marker, M1, knit to 2nd marker, M1, slip marker, knit to end.

Row 4: Sl 1, [knit to buttonhole marker, bind off 2 sts] 5 times, complete as for Row 2.

Row 5: Sl 1, knit across, casting on 2 sts at each buttonhole.

Row 6: Rep Row 2.

Bind off kwise on WS.

Finishing

Sew sleeves into armholes, sew sleeve and body seams. Sew buttons opposite buttonholes. Block lightly. ■

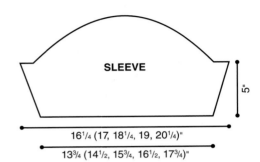

SLEEVE

5"

16¹/₄ (17, 18¹/₄, 19, 20¹/₄)"

13³/₄ (14¹/₂, 15³/₄, 16¹/₂, 17³/₄)"

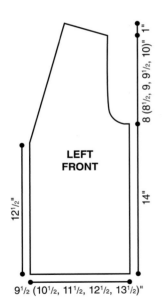

LEFT FRONT

8 (8¹/₂, 9, 9¹/₂, 10)" 1"

14"

12¹/₂"

9¹/₂ (10¹/₂, 11¹/₂, 12¹/₂, 13¹/₂)"

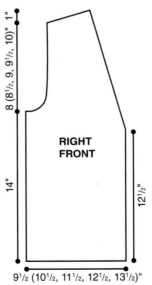

RIGHT FRONT

8 (8¹/₂, 9, 9¹/₂, 10)" 1"

14"

12¹/₂"

9¹/₂ (10¹/₂, 11¹/₂, 12¹/₂, 13¹/₂)"

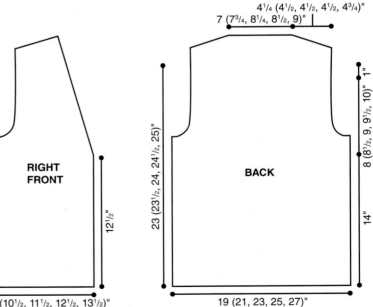

4¹/₄ (4¹/₂, 4¹/₂, 4¹/₂, 4³/₄)"

7 (7³/₄, 8¹/₄, 8¹/₂, 9)"

BACK

23 (23¹/₂, 24, 24¹/₂, 25)"

8 (8¹/₂, 9, 9¹/₂, 10)" 1"

14"

19 (21, 23, 25, 27)"

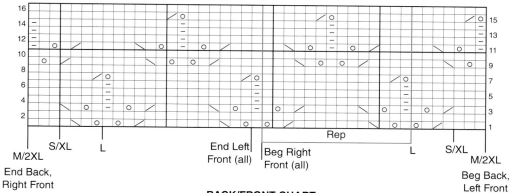

BACK/FRONT CHART

*Note: Pattern includes edge
sts not shown on chart.*

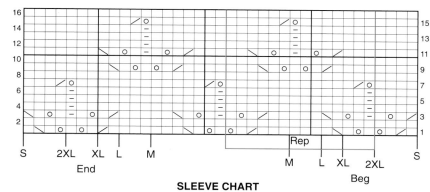

SLEEVE CHART

*Note: Pattern includes edge
sts not shown on chart.*

STITCH KEY
☐ K on RS, p on WS
⊟ P on RS, k on WS
⊡ Yo
⧄ K2tog
⧅ Ssk

ZIGGY'S ENSEMBLE

The zigzag pattern stitch is combined with sassy hues for babies who lead a colourful life.

Design | Celeste Pinheiro

Skill Level

INTERMEDIATE

Sizes

Top and Pants: Infant's 6 (12, 18, 24) months Instructions are given for smallest size, with larger sizes in parentheses. When only one number is given, it applies to all sizes.

Hat: Infant's 6–12 (18–24) months Instructions are given for smaller size, with larger size in parentheses. When only one number is given, it applies to both sizes.

Finished Measurements

Chest: 18 (20, 22, 24) inches
Pants waist: Approx 18 (20, 22, 24) inches
Hat circumference: Approx 18 (20) inches

Materials

DK weight yarn (136 yds/50g per ball):
  6 (7, 7, 8) balls pink (MC), 2 balls green (CC)
Size 4 (3.5mm) needles
Size 6 (4mm) straight and 2 double-point needles or size needed to obtain gauge
Size E/4 (3.5mm) crochet hook
½-inch button
¼-inch-wide elastic (for pants): approx 18 (20, 22, 24) inches

Gauge

20 sts = 4 inches/10cm in St st with larger needles
To save time, take time to check gauge.

Special Abbreviation

Slip, knit 2 together, pass (sk2p): Slip next st, k2tog, pass slipped st over k2tog and off needle to dec 2 sts.

Pattern Stitches

Eyelet Band (even number of sts)

Row 1 (WS): With smaller needles, knit.

Row 2: K1, *yo, k2tog; rep from * to last st, k1.

Row 3: Knit.

Chevron Lace (multiple of 6 sts + 2)

Row 1 (RS): K1, *yo, ssk, k4; rep from * to last st, k1.

Rows 2, 4 and 6: Purl.

Row 3: K1, *k1, yo, ssk, k1, k2tog, yo; rep from * to last st, k1.

Row 5: K1, *k2, yo, sk2p, yo, k1; rep from * to last st, k1.

Row 7: K1, *k3, yo, ssk, k1; rep from * to last st, k1.

Row 8: Purl.

Rep Rows 1–8 for pat.

I-Cord

Using 2 dpns, cast on 4 sts, do not turn; *slide sts to other end of needle, pull yarn across back, k4, rep from * until cord is desired length. Sl 1, k3tog, psso, fasten off.

Ziggy's Ensemble
Sample project was knit with
Jeannee DK (51 per cent
cotton/49 per cent acrylic)
from Plymouth Yarn Co.

Top

Back

With larger needles and MC, cast on 68 (74, 80, 86) sts. Work Rows 1–3 of Eyelet Band.

Change to larger needles, work 2 rows in St st, then work [Rows 1–8 of Chevron Lace] 4 (5, 6, 7) times, ending with a WS row. Continue in St st until back measures 5 (6, 7, 8) inches from beg, ending with a RS row and dec 22 (24, 26, 26) sts evenly over last row—46 (50, 54, 60) sts.

Beg with a WS row, work Rows 1–3 of Eyelet Band.

Shape armhole

Change to larger needles, work in St st, dec 1 st at each edge [every other row] 5 times—36 (40, 44, 50) sts.

Work even until back measures 2 inches above Eyelet Band, ending with a WS row.

Right Back

Knit across first 18 (20, 22, 25) sts, place rem 18 (20, 22, 25) sts on holder.

Continue in St st, and working 2 sts at centre back edge in garter st, work even until back measures 8½ (10, 11½, 13) inches from beg, ending with a WS row.

Shape neck

Work first 9 (9, 12, 13) sts, bind off 9 (11, 10, 12) sts at neck edge. Cut yarn.

With WS facing, attach yarn at neck edge, p1, p2tog, purl across—8 (8, 11, 12) sts rem.

Work even until back measures 9 (10½, 12, 13½) inches from beg, bind off all sts.

Left Back

Slip rem sts on needle. Beg with a RS row, attach yarn at centre back and work as for right back, keeping 2 sts at centre back in garter st until left back measures same as right back to neck, ending with a WS row.

Shape neck

Bind off 9 (11, 10, 12) sts at neck edge, k2tog, knit to end—8 (8, 11, 12) sts rem.

Work even until back measures 9 (10½, 12, 13½) inches from beg. Bind off all sts.

Back Ruffle

Hold with RS facing, with smaller needles and CC, pick up and knit 66 (72, 78, 84) sts across cast-on edge.

Change to larger needles.

Row 1 (WS): Purl.

Row 2: *K1, yo; rep from * to last st, k1—131 (143, 155, 167) sts.

Rows 3–7: Purl.

Bind off all sts.

Front

Work as for back, omitting centre back division, until front measures 7½ (9, 10½, 12) inches from beg, ending with a WS row.

Shape neck

Continuing in St st, k15 (16, 19, 20); attach 2nd ball of yarn and bind off centre 8 (8, 8, 10) sts; work to end. Continuing to work in St st, bind off at each neck edge [3 sts] once, [2 sts] 1 (2, 2, 2) time(s), then [dec 1 st] 1 (1, 0, 1) time(s)—8 (8, 11, 12) sts rem for each shoulder.

Work even until fronts measure 9 (10½, 12, 13½) inches from beg. Bind off shoulder sts.

Front Ruffle
Work front ruffle as for back ruffle.

Sleeve
With larger needles and MC, cast on 32 (32, 38, 44) sts. Beg and ending with a WS row, work Eyelet Band.

Change to larger needles, work 2 rows St st, then work [Rows 1–8 of Chevron Lace] twice, ending with a WS row.

Next row (RS): Knit.

Work Eyelet Band, ending with a WS row. Change to larger needles and continue in St st, *at the same time*, inc 1 st at each edge [every 4th row] 1 (4, 4, 3) time(s)—34 (40, 46, 50) sts.

Work even in St st until sleeve measures 3 (4, 5, 6) inches from beg, ending with a WS row.

Shape cap
Dec 1 st at each edge [every other row] 5 times—24 (30, 36, 40) sts.

Bind off rem sts.

Sleeve Ruffle
Hold with RS facing, with smaller needles and CC, pick up and knit 30 (30, 36, 42) sts across cast-on edge, work as for back—59 (59, 71, 83) sts at end of Row 2.

Assembly
Sew shoulder, armhole, sleeve and side seams.

Neckband
Hold with RS facing, with smaller needles and MC, pick up and knit 53 (57, 57, 61) sts around neckline.

Knit 3 rows.

Next row (RS): *K2tog, yo; rep from * to last st, k1.

Knit 1 row, bind off loosely. Without cutting yarn, using crochet hook, make a chain-st button loop (see Crochet Basics on page 25), fasten off and sew end to neck edge. Sew button opposite at back neck.

Waist Cord
With larger dpn and CC, work I-cord approx 38 (40, 42, 44) inches long. Thread through eyelet row at waist and tie into bow at centre front.

Pants

Left Leg
With larger needles and MC, cast on 56 (62, 68, 74) sts. Work lace border (Eyelet Band, [Rows 1–8 of Chevron Lace] twice, Eyelet Band) as for sleeve, ending with a WS row. Change to larger needles, work in St st until leg measures 3 (5, 6, 7) inches from beg, ending with a WS row.

Shape crotch
Bind off 6 sts at beg of next 2 rows—44 (50, 56, 62) sts.

Work even until leg measures 1 (1½, 2, 2½) inch(es) above crotch shaping, ending with a WS row.

Short-row shaping
[K22 (25, 28, 31), bring yarn to front, slip next st, take yarn to back, turn and purl back on WS; work 4 rows in St st across all sts, working wrap tog with wrapped st] 4 times.

Work even until leg measures 6½ (7, 7½, 8) inches from crotch shaping on left side (this edge will be at centre front seam), ending with a RS row.

Beg with a WS row, work 7 rows in St st.

Next row (WS): Change to smaller needles, knit across (fold line for waistband).

Work 6 rows in St st, bind off all sts.

Leg Ruffle
Hold with RS facing, with smaller needles and CC, pick up and knit 54 (60, 66, 72) sts across cast-on edge. Work leg ruffle as for back ruffle—107 (119, 131, 143) sts at end of Row 2.

Right Leg
Work as for left leg to beg of short-row shaping, ending with a RS row.

Short-row shaping
[P22 (25, 28, 31), bring yarn to front, slip next st, take yarn to back, turn and knit back on RS; work 4 rows St st across all sts, working wrap tog with wrapped st] 4 times.

Work even until leg measures 6½ (7, 7½, 8) inches from crotch shaping on RS (this edge will be at centre front seam), ending with a RS row.

Complete as for left leg.

Assembly
Sew inseams, centre front, centre back and crotch seams. Adjust elastic to fit waist, overlap ends and sew tog. Trim excess. Fold waistband over elastic and sew in place.

With larger dpns and CC, work I-cord for approx 28 inches, thread through 2nd Eyelet Band of left leg, tie in bow at knee.

Hat
With larger needles and MC, cast on 84 (96) sts. Work lace border as for sleeve (Eyelet Band, [Rows 1–8 of Chevron Lace] twice, Eyelet Band), ending with a WS row.

Next row (size 6–12 months): [K19, k2tog] 4 times—80 sts.

Purl 1 row.

Shape top
Row 1 (both sizes): [K8 (10), k2tog] 8 times—72 (88) sts.

Row 2 and rem WS rows: Purl.

Row 3: [K7 (9), k2tog] 8 times—64, (80) sts.

Continue to dec as above, having 1 less knit st between decs until 8 sts rem. Cut yarn, leaving a 12-inch end, and thread through rem sts.

Hat Ruffle
Hold with RS facing, with smaller needles and CC, pick up and knit 84 (96) sts across cast-on edge. Work as for back ruffle—167 (191) sts at end of Row 2.

Assembly
Sew seam. ■

7 (8, 9, 10)"

SLEEVE

3 (4, 5, 6)"

1"

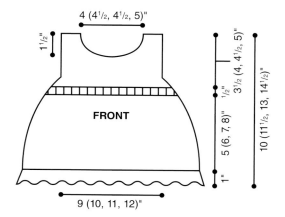

4 (4 1/2, 4 1/2, 5)"

1 1/2"

3 1/2 (4, 4 1/2, 5)"
1/2"
10 (11 1/2, 13, 14 1/2)"

FRONT

5 (6, 7, 8)"
1"

9 (10, 11, 12)"

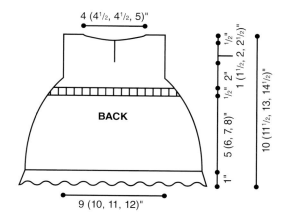

4 (4 1/2, 4 1/2, 5)"

1/2"
1 (1 1/2, 2, 2 1/2)"
1/2"
2"
10 (11 1/2, 13, 14 1/2)"

BACK

5 (6, 7, 8)"
1"

9 (10, 11, 12)"

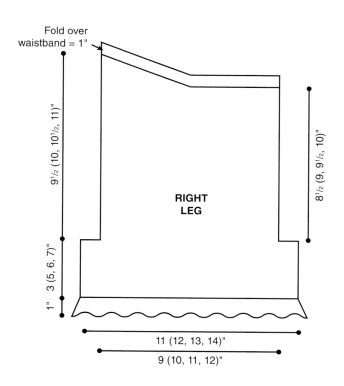

Fold over waistband = 1"

9 1/2 (10, 10 1/2, 11)"

8 1/2 (9, 9 1/2, 10)"

RIGHT LEG

1"
3 (5, 6, 7)"

11 (12, 13, 14)"
9 (10, 11, 12)"

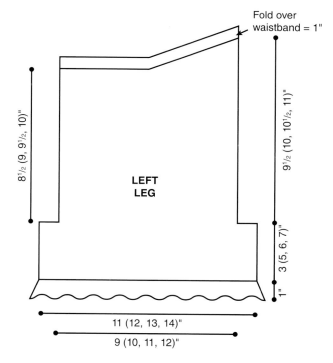

Fold over waistband = 1"

8 1/2 (9, 9 1/2, 10)"

9 1/2 (10, 10 1/2, 11)"

LEFT LEG

1"
3 (5, 6, 7)"

11 (12, 13, 14)"
9 (10, 11, 12)"

DIAGONAL EYELETS BABY SET

This clever lace pattern is perfect for welcoming Baby into our world. The eyelets in the jacket also serve as the buttonholes.

Design | Kennita Tully

Skill Level

INTERMEDIATE

Sizes

Infant's 6 (12, 18) months Instructions are given for smallest size, with larger sizes in parentheses. When only one number is given, it applies to all sizes.

Finished Measurements

Blanket: 30 x 35 inches
Jacket chest: 24½ (27½, 30½) inches
Jacket length: 11 (12, 13) inches
Hat circumference: Approx 15 inches

Materials

DK weight yarn (86 yds/50g per ball):
  5 (5, 6) balls green/purple multi
Size 6 (4mm) straight and 36-inch circular
  needles or size needed to obtain gauge
Stitch markers
4 (¾-inch) buttons

Gauge

19 sts and 28 rows = 4 inches/10cm in Diagonal Eyelets pat
To save time, take time to check gauge.

Pattern Stitches

Diagonal Eyelets

Version A (multiple of 10 sts + 7)

Row 1 (RS): K1, *yo, ssk, k3, p5; rep from * to last 6 sts, end yo, ssk, k4.

Rows 2, 4, 6 and 8: K1, *p5, k5; rep from * to last 6 sts, end p5, k1.

Row 3: K1, *k1, yo, ssk, k2, p5; rep from * to last 6 sts, end k1, yo, ssk, k3.

Row 5: K1, *k2, yo, ssk, k1, p5; rep from * to last 6 sts, end k2, yo, ssk, k2.

Row 7: K1, *k3, yo, ssk, p5; rep from * to last 6 sts, end k3, yo, ssk, k1.

Row 9: K1, *p5, k3, k2tog, yo; rep from * to last 6 sts, end p5, k1.

Rows 10, 12, 14 and 16: K1, *k5, p5; rep from * to last 6 sts, end k6.

Row 11: K1, *p5, k2, k2tog, yo, k1; rep from * to last 6 sts, end p5, k1.

Row 13: K1, *p5, k1, k2tog, yo, k2; rep from * to last 6 sts, end p5, k1.

Row 15: K1, *p5, k2tog, yo, k3; rep from * to last 6 sts, end p5, k1.

Rep Rows 1–16 for pat.

Version B (multiple of 10 sts + 2)

Row 1 (RS): K1, *yo, ssk, k3, p5; rep from * to last st, end k1.

Rows 2, 4, 6 and 8: K1, *k5, p5; rep from * to last st, end k1.

Diagonal Eyelets Baby Set
Sample project was knit with Linen Isle
(50 per cent cotton/30 per cent rayon/
20 per cent linen) from Plymouth Yarn Co.

Row 3: K1, *k1, yo, ssk, k2, p5; rep from * to last st, end k1.

Row 5: K1, *k2, yo, ssk, k1, p5; rep from * to last st, end k1.

Row 7: K1, *k3, yo, ssk, p5; rep from * to last st, end k1.

Row 9: K1, *p5, k3, k2tog, yo; rep from * to last st, end k1.

Rows 10, 12, 14 and 16: K1, *p5, k5; rep from * to last st, end k1.

Row 11: K1, *p5, k2, k2tog, yo, k1; rep from * to last st, end k1.

Row 13: K1, *p5, k1, k2tog, yo, k2; rep from * to last st, end k1.

Row 15: K1, *p5, k2tog, yo, k3; rep from * to last st, end k1.

Rep Rows 1–16 for pat.

Blanket

Note
Circular needle is used to accommodate large number of stitches. Do not join; work in rows.

Blanket
With circular needle and using long-tail cast-on method (see page 26), cast on 137 sts.

Knit 3 rows.

Following Version A, work 15 reps of Diagonal Eyelets pat, then work Rows 1–8 once more.

Knit 4 rows.

Bind off.

Finishing
With circular needle, pick up and knit 194 sts along side edge, and then work in garter st for 3 rows. Bind off. Rep for other side edge. Weave in all ends. Wash and pin to measurements.

Jacket

Back
Using long-tail cast-on method (see page 26), cast on 57 (62, 67) sts.

Set up pat (WS): Following Version A (B, A) of Diagonal Eyelets pat, work Row 2.

Continue with Rows 1–16 of pat as established for 6 (6½, 7) inches; mark edges for armhole placement.

Continue in pat until piece measures 11 (12, 13) inches, ending with Row 8 or 16.

Bind off all sts.

Fronts
Make 2

Cast on 32 (37, 42) sts.

Set up pat: Following Version B (A, B) of Diagonal Eyelets pat, work Row 2.

Continue with Rows 1–16 of pat as established until piece measures same as back, marking armhole placement as for back.

Bind off all sts.

Sleeves
Using long-tail cast-on method (see page 26), cast on 27 sts.

Set up pat: Following Version A of Diagonal Eyelets pat, work Row 2.

Work Rows 1–8, and then change to St st for rest of sleeve.

At the same time, inc 1 st each side on 2nd RS row, then [every 4 (4, 2) rows] 5 (11, 3) times, then [every 6 (0, 4) rows] 4 (0, 11) times—47 (51, 57) sts.

Work until sleeve measures approx 8 (8½, 9) inches.

Bind off all sts.

Finishing
Wash and block pieces to measurements.

Mark shoulders by placing markers 2½ (2¾, 3) inches to left and right of centre back. Sew shoulder seams between armhole edges and markers, matching pattern.

Sew in sleeves between armhole markers.

Sew sleeve and side seams.

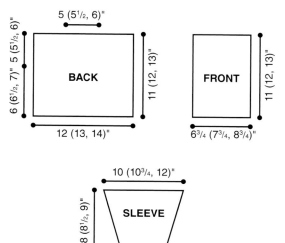

Fold back and tack collar down.

Sew on buttons, using the eyelets as buttonholes.

Hat
Cast on 72 sts.

Set up pat: Following Version B of Diagonal Eyelets pat, work Row 2.

Work Rows 1–8 in pat as established.

Work even in St st until piece measures 3½ inches from beg.

Shape crown
Set-up row (RS): K1, *k8, k2tog, place marker; rep from *, end k1—65 sts.

Next row: Purl.

Dec row (RS): *Knit to 2 sts before marker, k2tog; rep from * to last st, k1—58 sts.

Rep dec row [every other row] 7 times—9 sts.

Cut yarn, leaving a 12-inch tail.

Using tapestry needle, weave tail through rem sts and pull tight.

Using tail, sew seam.

Weave in all ends. ■

EBONY ELEGANCE

Nipped at the waist and kissed with lace, our jacket is sure to please.

Design | Tabetha Hedrick

Skill Level

INTERMEDIATE

Sizes

Woman's small (medium, large, extra large, 2X-large) Instructions are given for smallest size, with larger sizes in parentheses. When only one number is given, it applies to all sizes.

Finished Measurements

Chest (buttoned): 35 (38½, 43½, 49½, 51) inches
Length: 21¼ (22½, 23¼, 24, 24¾) inches

Materials

DK weight yarn (240 yds/100g per ball):
  6 (6, 7, 8, 8) balls black
Size 6 (4mm) straight and 32-inch circular needles
  or size needed to obtain gauge
Stitch holder
5 (¾-inch) buttons

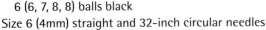

Gauge

23 sts and 38 rows = 4 inches/10cm in Woven St pat (blocked)
20 sts and 30 rows = 4 inches/10cm in Diamond Lace pat (blocked)
To save time, take time to check gauge.

Pattern Stitches

Woven St (even number of sts)

Row 1 (RS): Sl 1, k1, *sl 1 wyif, k1; rep from * across.

Row 2: Sl 1, purl across.

Row 3: Sl 1, k2, *sl 1 wyif; rep from * to last st, end k1.

Row 4: Sl 1, purl across.

Rep Rows 1–4 for pat.

Diamond Lace (multiple of 10 sts + 2)

Row 1 (RS): Sl 1, *k2, k2tog, yo, k1, yo, ssk, k3; rep from * to last st, end k1.

Row 2 and all even-numbered rows: Sl 1, purl across.

Row 3: Sl 1, *k1, k2tog, yo, k3, yo, ssk, k2; rep from * to last st, end k1.

Row 5: Sl 1, *k2tog, yo, k2tog, yo, k1, yo, ssk, yo, ssk, k1; rep from * to last st, end k1.

Row 7: Sl 1, *yo, k2tog, yo, k3, yo, ssk, yo, k3tog; rep from * to last st, end k1.

Row 9: Sl 1, *k8, ssk, yo; rep from * to last st, end k1.

Row 11: Sl 1, *yo, ssk, k5, k2tog, yo, k1; rep from * to last st, end k1.

Row 13: Sl 1, *k1, yo, ssk, k3, k2tog, yo, k2; rep from * to last st, end k1.

Row 15: Sl 1, *yo, ssk, yo, ssk, k1, k2tog, yo, k2tog, yo, k1; rep from * to last st, end k1.

Row 17: Sl 1, *k1, yo, ssk, yo, k3tog, yo, k2tog, yo, k2; rep from * to last st, end k1.

Row 19: Sl 1, *k3, ssk, yo, k5; rep from * to last st, end k1.

Row 20: Sl 1, purl across.

Rep Rows 1–20 for pat.

Notes

Work all increases and decreases 1 stitch in from edge. Work slip, slip, knit (ssk) at the beginning of the row and knit 2 together (k2tog) at the end.

Chart is included for those preferring to work Diamond Lace pattern from a chart.

Jacket

Back

Cast on 92 (102, 112, 122, 132) sts. Purl 1 row.

[Work Rows 1–20 of Diamond Lace pat] 3 times.

Knit next RS row, inc 12 (10, 12, 22, 20) sts evenly across—104 (112, 124, 144, 152) sts.

Next row (WS): Sl 1, k1, p2, *k2, p2; rep from * across.

Rep last row for ribbed waist until ribbing measures 2¾ inches, ending with a WS row.

Change to Woven St pat and work even until back measures 13¼ (14¼, 14¾, 15¼, 15½) inches.

Shape armhole

Maintaining Woven St pat, bind off 6 (6, 8, 12, 12) sts at beg of next 2 rows, then dec 1 st at each edge [every other row] 6 (7, 8, 11, 12) times—80 (86, 92, 98, 104) sts.

Work even in pat until armhole measures 7¼ (7½, 7¾, 8, 8½) inches, ending with a WS row.

Shape shoulders

Bind off 4 (5, 5, 6, 6) sts at beg of next 6 rows, then bind off 7 (6, 8, 6, 8) sts at beg of next 2 rows. Place rem 42 (44, 48, 50, 52) back neck sts on a holder.

Right Front

Cast on 52 (52, 62, 72, 72) sts. Purl 1 row.

[Work Rows 1–20 of Diamond Lace pat] 3 times.

Knit next RS row, dec 0 (0, 2, 4, 4) sts evenly across— 52 (52, 60, 68, 68) sts.

Next row (WS): Sl 1, k1, p2, *k2, p2; rep from * across.

Rep last row for ribbed waist until ribbing measures 2¾ inches, ending with a WS row.

Change to Woven St pat and work even until front measures 13¼ (14¼, 14¾, 15¼, 15½) inches, ending with a RS row.

Shape armhole & neck

Note: Read through front instructions before beg; neckline shaping is worked at the same time as armhole shaping.

On next row (WS), bind off 6 (6, 8, 12, 12) sts. Purl across.

Maintaining Woven St pat throughout, beg on this row, dec 1 st at end of row [every RS row] 6 (7, 8, 11, 12) times for armhole, and *at the same time*, dec 1 st at beg of row [every other row] 10 (13, 18, 11, 2) times, then [every 4th row] 9 (8, 6, 10, 16) times for neck—19 (21, 22, 24, 26) sts.

Work even until armhole measures 7¼ (7½, 7¾, 8, 8½) inches, ending with a RS row.

Shape shoulders
Bind off 4 (5, 5, 6, 6) sts at beg of next 6 rows, then bind off rem 7 (6, 8, 6, 8) sts.

Left Front
Cast on 52 (52, 62, 72, 72) sts. Purl 1 row.

[Work rows 1–20 of Diamond Lace pat] 3 times.

Knit next RS row, dec 0 (0, 2, 4, 4) sts evenly across—52 (52, 60, 68, 68) sts.

Next row (WS): Sl 1, k1, p2, *k2, p2; rep from * across.

Rep last row for ribbed waist until ribbing measures 2¾ inches, ending with a WS row.

Change to Woven St pat and work even until front measures 13¼ (14¼, 14¾, 15¼, 15½) inches, ending with a WS row.

Shape armhole & neck
Note: Read through front instructions before beg; neckline shaping is worked at the same time as armhole shaping.

On next row (RS), bind off 6 (6, 8, 12, 12) sts. Continue Woven St pat for 2 rows.

Maintaining Woven St pat throughout, beg on this row, dec 1 st at beg of row [every RS row] 6 (7, 8, 11, 12) times for armhole, and *at the same time*, dec 1 st at end of row [every other row] 10 (13, 18, 11, 2) times, then [every 4th row] 9 (8, 6, 10, 16) times for neck—19 (16, 22, 24, 26) sts.

Work even until armhole measures 7¼ (7½, 7¾, 8, 8½) inches, ending with a WS row.

Shape shoulders
Bind off 4 (5, 5, 6, 6) sts at beg of next 6 rows, then bind off rem 7 (6, 8, 6, 8) sts.

Sleeves
Cast on 54 (54, 54, 58, 58) sts.

Rows 1–10: Sl 1, *k2, p2; rep from * to last st, end k1.

Change to Woven St pat, inc 1 st at each edge [every 16 (12, 10, 8, 6) rows] 9 (3, 7, 8, 7) times, then [every 0 (14, 12, 10, 8) rows] 0 (8, 7, 9, 14) times, working added sts into pat—72 (76, 82, 92, 100) sts.

Work even in pat until sleeve measures 17½ (18, 18½, 18½, 18½) from beg.

Shape cap
Bind off 6 (6, 8, 12, 12) sts at beg of next 2 rows. Maintaining pat, dec 1 st at each edge [every 4th row] 2 (1, 2, 3, 0) time(s), then every other row 19 (22, 19, 17, 24) times. Bind off rem 18 (18, 24, 28, 28) sts.

Assembly
Block pieces to measurements.

Sew shoulder seams.

Mark positions for 5 buttonholes along right front edge, with first 1 inch from bottom edge, last at beg of neck shaping and rem 3 spaced evenly between.

Front Band

With circular needle, RS facing, pick up and knit 68 (68, 76, 76, 80) sts along right front edge, 39 (39, 40, 43, 44) sts along right front neck, 42 (44, 48, 50, 52) sts across back neck, 39 (39, 40, 43, 44) sts along left front neck, 68 (68, 76, 76, 80) sts along left front edge—256 (258, 280, 288, 300) sts.

Beg k2, p2 rib

Rows 1 and 3 (WS): K1, *p2, k2; rep from * to last 3 sts, end p2, k1.

Row 2: P1, *k2, p2; rep from * to last 3 sts, end k2, p1.

Row 4 (buttonhole row): Work in rib to first marked buttonhole position (ending with 2 purl sts), k2tog, yo, rib to end, making 4 more buttonholes as marked.

Work 4 more rows in rib pat. Bind off in rib.

Sew side and sleeve seams. Sew buttons opposite buttonholes. Block lightly to finished measurements. ■

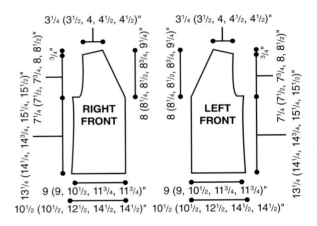

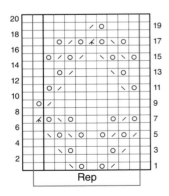

STITCH KEY
☐ K on RS, p on WS
⊡ Yo
◪ K2tog
◩ Ssk
◪ K3tog

DIAMOND LACE CHART

Note: *The first sl st at beg of each row is not shown on the chart.*

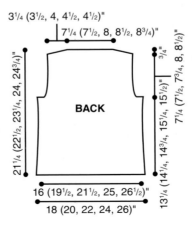

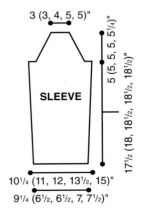

LACY BABY CARDIGAN

What is sweeter than a baby in lace and ribbons?

Design | Silka Burgoyne

Skill Level

INTERMEDIATE

Sizes

Infant's 6 (12, 24) months Instructions are given for smallest size, with larger sizes in parentheses. When only one number is given, it applies to all sizes.

Finished Measurements

Chest: 20 (22, 24¼) inches
Length: 10½ (12¼, 13½) inches

Materials

DK weight yarn (130 yds/50g per ball):
 3 (3, 4) balls red
Size 3 (3.25mm) 32-inch or longer circular
 needle
Size 5 (3.75mm) 32-inch or longer circular needle and set of double-point needles or size needed to obtain gauge
Stitch markers
Stitch holders
2 yds ³⁄₁₆- or ¼-inch-wide ribbon for sleeves and
 neckband
1 small hook-and-eye set

Gauge

24 sts and 30 rows = 4 inches/10cm in Dot St pat with larger needles (blocked)
To save time, take time to check gauge.

Pattern Stitches

Foaming Waves (multiple of 12 sts + 1)

Rows 1–4: Sl 1, knit across.

Row 5: K1, *k2tog twice, [yo, k1] 3 times, yo, ssk twice, k1; rep from * across.

Row 6: Purl across.

Rows 7–12: Rep [Rows 5 and 6] 3 times.

Rep Rows 1–12 for pat.

Note: When working in rnds, purl Rnds 2 and 4, knit Rnds 6, 8, 10 and 12.

Dot St (multiple of 4 sts)

Row 1: *P1, k3; rep from * across.

Row 2: Purl across.

Row 3: *K1, p1, k2; rep from * across.

Row 4: Purl across.

Rep Rows 1–4 for pat.

Note: When working in rnds, knit Rnds 2 and 4.

Seed St (even number of sts)

Row 1: *K1, p1; rep from * across.

Rep Row 1 for pat.

Notes

Always slip first stitch of every row purlwise, knit last stitch on right-side (RS) rows, purl last stitch on wrong-side (WS) rows.

Sleeve instructions are written using Magic Loop Method (see page 123), OR you may use double-point needles if you prefer.

Charts are provided for those preferring to work the Foaming Waves and Dot St patterns from a chart.

Cardigan

Body

With smaller circular needle, cast on 110 (122, 134) sts.

Change to larger needle, slip first st, work Foaming Waves pat across rem sts, place marker, end k1. [Work Rows 1–12 of pat between markers] 3 (4, 4) times, then rep Rows 1–4. Body should measure approx 5½ (7, 7) inches.

Beg working Dot St pat, placing marker after first st and before last st, always slip first st and knit (RS) or purl (WS) last st until body measures 6 (7½, 8½) inches, ending with a WS row.

Divide for fronts & back

With RS facing, slip first 27 (30, 33) sts on a holder, join yarn and work centre 56 (62, 68) for back in Dot St pat, slip rem 27 (30, 33) sts onto another holder.

Back

Working on back sts, bind off 1 (2, 3) st(s) at beg of next 2 rows, then continue in Dot St pat as established until body measures approx 10½ (12¼, 13½) inches, ending with a WS row—54 (58, 62) sts.

On next RS row, slip first 14 (14, 15) sts to a holder, bind off centre 28 (30, 32) sts, and slip rem 14 (14, 15) sts onto another holder.

Right Front

With RS facing, join yarn at centre front, work to underarm. Continue to work in established pat, binding off 1 (2, 3) st(s) at beg of next row, and *at the same time*, when front measures 6 (8¼, 8½) inches, shape neck by dec 1 st [every row] 9 (10, 2) times, then [every other row] 4 (4, 13) times—13 (14, 15) sts.

Work even until front measures same as back to shoulder. Slip shoulder sts to a holder.

Left Front

With RS facing, join yarn at armhole edge, bind off 1 (2, 3) st(s), complete row in pat. Continue to work in established pat and *at the same time*, when front measures 6 (8¼, 8½) inches, shape neck by dec 1 st [every row] 9 (10, 2) times, then [every other row] 4 (4, 13) times—13 (14, 15) sts.

Work even until front measures same as back to shoulder. Slip shoulder sts to a holder.

Bind off front and back shoulders, using 3-needle bind-off (see page 27).

Sleeves

With larger circular needle, RS facing, pick up and knit 50 (52, 56) sts around arm opening; do not pick up sts from bound-off sts and do not join at this point. Turn and purl across, then pick up and knit 1 st in bound-off st, turn, with RS facing for next row. Work in Dot St pat and knit picked-up st, pick up and knit 1 st in bound-off st on other side, turn. Work in this manner until sts have been picked up in all bound-off sts. After last st is picked up,

Lacy Baby Cardigan
Sample project was knit with Cotton
Bam Boo (52 per cent cotton/48 per cent
bamboo viscose) from Classic Elite Yarns.

join, mark beg of rnd, and work pat in rnds, making sure to purl Rnds 2 and 4. Work 1 rnd.

Shape sleeves by dec 1 st on each side of marker [every other rnd] 4 (2, 0) times, [every 4th rnd] 6 (8, 10) times, then [every 6th round] 0 (0, 1) time(s)—32 (36, 40) sts rem. Work even until sleeve measures approx 5 (6, 7) inches.

Sleeve Band

Rnd 1: Purl.

Rnd 2: Knit.

Rnd 3: *K2tog, yo, k2 (1, 2); rep from * around.

Rnd 4: Knit.

Rnd 5: Purl.

Rnd 6: Knit.

Rnd 7: Knit into front and back of every st—64 (72, 80) sts.

Rnds 8 and 9: Rep Rnds 6 and 7—128 (144, 160) sts.

Sleeve should measure approx 6 (7, 8) inches. Bind off all sts.

Neckband

With smaller circular needle, RS facing, beg at lower right front, pick up and knit 34 (44, 50) sts to first neck dec, place marker, 24 (27, 30) sts along neck edge, 28 (30, 32) sts across back neck, 24 (27, 30) sts along left neck edge, place marker, 34 (44, 50) sts along left front—144 (172, 192) sts.

Row 1 (WS): *P1, k1; rep from * across.

Row 2 (6 months only): Work in established Seed St to first marker, slip marker, *p2tog, yo; rep from * to 2nd marker, work in established Seed St to end.

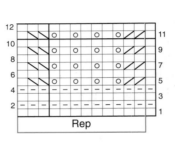

FOAMING WAVES CHART

STITCH KEY
☐ K on RS, p on WS
⊟ P on RS, k on WS
⊙ Yo
⧄ K2tog
⧅ Ssk

DOT STITCH CHART

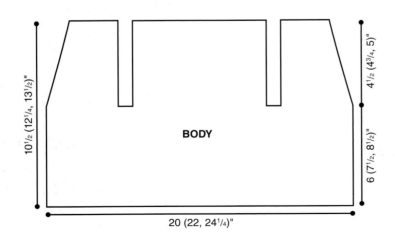

BODY

10½ (12¼, 13½)"

4½ (4¾, 5)"

6 (7½, 8½)"

20 (22, 24¼)"

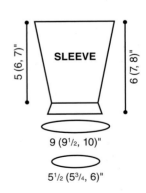

SLEEVE

5 (6, 7)"

6 (7, 8)"

9 (9½, 10)"

5½ (5¾, 6)"

Row 2 (12 and 24 months only): Work in established Seed St to first marker, slip marker, *p1, yo, p2tog, k1, yo, k2tog; rep from * to next marker, slip marker, complete row in Seed St.

Row 3 (all sizes): Work in established Seed St.

Bind off all sts in pat.

Sew hook-and-eye closure at beg of neck shaping. Referring to photo, thread ribbon through neck and sleeve bands. ■

Magic Loop

This method of working in the round uses one long circular needle, ideally one with a very flexible cable.

Cast on or pick up the required number of stitches onto a 29-inch, or longer, circular needle. Slide the stitches to the cable portion of the needle. Pinch the cable in half and then pull to create a large loop. Arrange half the stitches on one needle tip, and half on the other.

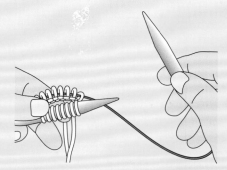

Follow These 3 Easy Steps

1. The illustration to the right shows how your stitches should look after you have distributed them on the two parts of the needle. The points of the needle and the "tail" from the cast-on row are facing to the right and the cables are on your left.

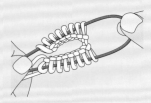

2. The next illustration shows how to begin working your first round: Hold the needle in your left hand, and pull out the needle that holds the "tail end"; the stitches that were on the needle point are now resting on the cable. Begin working the stitches that are still on the opposite needle point as if you were working on straight needles.

3. At the end of the row, simply turn the work around and reposition the stitches. Once again, the needles are pointing to the right, and the cable loop is to the left. Continue to work in this manner until desired length is reached.

The examples show how the work will appear on the needles as the work gets longer.

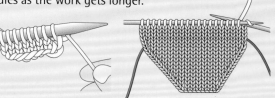

INDEX

First Steps

Cables & Lace Dishcloth, 30

Suri Lace Scarf, 34

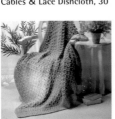

Candles Triangular Scarf, 36

Blueberry Lace, 39

Gossamer Lace Evening
Wrap, 32

Irish Net Valance, 42

Make Mine Colourful
Throw, 44

Catching On

Easy Lace Cowl, 46

Evening Out, 48

Simple Lace Top, 51

Snow Bunny Cardigan, 54

Buttercup Baby Set, 58

Natural Beauty for Baby, 62

INDEX

GENERAL INFORMATION

Metric Conversion Charts

INCHES INTO MILLIMETRES & CENTIMETRES (Rounded off slightly)

inches	mm	cm	inches	cm	inches	cm	inches	cm
1/8	3	0.3	5	12.5	21	53.5	38	96.5
1/4	6	0.6	5 1/2	14.0	22	56.0	39	99.0
3/8	10	1.0	6	15.0	23	58.5	40	101.5
1/2	13	1.3	7	18.0	24	61.0	41	104.0
5/8	15	1.5	8	20.5	25	63.5	42	106.5
3/4	20	2.0	9	23.0	26	66.0	43	109.0
7/8	22	2.2	10	25.5	27	68.5	44	112.0
1	25	2.5	11	28.0	28	71.0	45	114.5
1 1/4	32	3.2	12	30.5	29	73.5	46	117.0
1 1/2	38	3.8	13	33.0	30	76.0	47	119.5
1 3/4	45	4.5	14	35.5	31	79.0	48	122.0
2	50	5.0	15	38.0	32	81.5	49	124.5
2 1/2	65	6.5	16	40.5	33	84.0	50	127.0
3	75	7.5	17	43.0	34	86.5		
3 1/2	90	9.0	18	46.0	35	89.0		
4	100	10.0	19	48.5	36	91.5		
4 1/2	115	11.5	20	51.0	37	94.0		

METRIC CONVERSIONS

yards	x	.9144	=	metres (m)
yards	x	91.44	=	centimetres (cm)
inches	x	2.54	=	centimetres (cm)
inches	x	25.40	=	millimetres (mm)
inches	x	.0254	=	metres (m)

centimetres	x	.3937	=	inches
metres	x	1.0936	=	yards

KNITTING NEEDLES CONVERSION CHART

U.S.	0	1	2	3	4	5	6	7	8	9	10	10½	11	13	15
Canada/U.K.	14	13	12	10	-	9	8	7	6	5	4	3	0	00	000
Metric (mm)	2	2.25	2.75	3.25	3.5	3.75	4	4.5	5	5.5	6	6.5	8	9	10

CROCHET HOOKS CONVERSION CHART

U.S.	1/B	2/C	3/D	4/E	5/F	6/G	8/H	9/I	10/J	10½/K	15/N
Canada/U.K.	13	-	10	9	-	8	6	5	4	3	000
Metric (mm)	2.25	2.75	3.25	3.5	3.75	4	5	5.5	6	6.5	10

Skill Levels

BEGINNER

Projects for first-time knitters using basic knit and purl stitches. Minimal shaping.

EASY

Projects using basic stitches, repetitive stitch patterns, simple colour changes and simple shaping and finishing.

INTERMEDIATE

Projects with a variety of stitches, such as basic cables and lace, simple intarsia, double-pointed needles and knitting-in-the-round needle techniques, mid-level shaping and finishing.

EXPERIENCED

Projects using advanced techniques and stitches, such as short rows, Fair Isle, more intricate intarsia, cables, lace patterns and numerous colour changes.

GOT A PASSION FOR CRAFTING?

Each craft pattern book offers unique designs, easy-to-follow instructions, helpful how-to illustrations and full-colour photos—all for a very low price! Get creative and start a beautiful new project today for yourself or a loved one.

Crocheting Slippers
Crocheting Slippers provides 18 delightful patterns for cute and cozy slippers to keep the whole family's toes toasty. A handy stitch guide helps you put together these creative designs.

Crocheting Toys
In an age where so many things are mass-produced, the craft of crochet allows you to custom-create a toy or game for that special little one. These handcrafted toys will quickly become favourites and heartfelt reminders in years to come.

Quilting Pot Holders
Add flare to your kitchen with 45 unique designs for handy pot holders—you're sure to find something to suit any taste! *Quilting Pot Holders* includes full-colour photos of each project, useful instructions, templates and patterns.

Knitting for Dogs
Dogs are beloved members of our families, so of course we want to make them feel important with their own sweaters, beds and comfort toys. These fun designs will be a perfect match for your four-footed friend.

Sewing Aprons
Like to cook and love to sew? Just select one of our easy designs for fun and funky aprons that will keep your clothes clean while you're busy in the kitchen or the garden. Start sewing now, and stitch one for yourself or for a special friend!

Knitting Winter Accessories
Keep toasty warm when the cold winds blow with this great collection of knitted accessories. You'll find cozy hats, classy scarves, plus mittens and fingerless gloves. It's time to start knitting for a warm winter ahead.

Look for Company's Coming cookbooks and craft books in stores or order them on-line at

www.companyscoming.com